Royal Fireworks   Language Arts   by Michael Clay Thompson

Caesar's English 1

The Latin Foundation of English Vocabulary for Elementary Scholars

Second Edition
Revised and Expanded
January 2011

Michael Clay Thompson
and
Myriam Borges Thompson

Royal Fireworks Press
Unionville, New York

Other Works By
Michael Clay Thompson

The Word Within The Word

The Magic Lens

Thinkers

Classic Words

Classics In The Classroom

Opus 40

Advanced Academic Writing

Grammar Voyage

Royal Fireworks Press
First Ave, PO Box 399
Unionville NY 10988
845 726 4444
Fax 845 726 3824
Email: mail@rfwp.com
Website: rfwp.com

ISBN 13: 978-0-8802-209-8

Printed and bound in the United States of America by American citizens using recycled, acid-free paper, vegetable-based inks, and environmentally-friendly cover coatings at the Royal Fireworks Printing Company of Unionville, New York.

Table of Contents

Caesar's English

Once upon a time...far, far away...

Long ago, far from our New World, a great warrior civilization lived and died. Throughout the ancient world, they built roads, made laws, and wrote literature. Today, their great buildings have crumbled to dusty ruins, but echoes of their words are still heard because the English language (and others, such as Spanish) uses remnants of their language, Latin.

The vanished civilization, of course, was Rome, in Italy, and Rome rose to power over 2,000 years ago, which is more than twenty centuries.

Only 500 years ago, astonished Europeans discovered that there was an inhabited New World on the back side of the earth, and the Age of Exploration was on. Often neglected in our thoughts about these centuries is the dominant role of Spain—the oldest European settlements in this hemisphere were Spanish, the oldest city, St. Augustine, was Spanish, and the oldest documents in the United States were written in Spanish. Many cities and towns in the United States retain their Spanish names today.

After three centuries of conflict and exploration a new nation—as Abraham Lincoln put it—was conceived on this continent.

In the 200 years since, this new nation—the United States—has conceived a new kind of English, which is a combination of Roman Latin, ancient Greek, German Anglo-Saxon, Spanish, American Indian, and many other tongues. Walt Whitman, the poet of *Leaves of Grass*, once wrote:

> Thus far, impress'd by New England writers and schoolmasters, we tacitly abandon ourselves to the notion that our United States have been fashion'd from the British islands only, and essentially form a second England only— which is a very great mistake...To that composite American identity of the future, Spanish character will supply some of the most needed parts.

But even with all of these influences, Latin, the language of ancient Rome, is still the most important source of English words.

In this book, we will learn about our own English by learning about the Latin remnants inside it.

Remnants? Yes. Many of our words are made of two or three fragments of Latin. We sometimes call these pieces *prefixes*, *suffixes*, or *stems*, but to make things easy, we will usually just call them *stems*.

The stem **sub**, for example, is part of many English words. **Sub** means under, and we find **sub** in words like *submarine*, *submerge*, and *subtract*. We also find sub in harder words, such as *subterranean*, *subordinate*, *substantial*, and even *subterfuge*.

Even though words like these seem hard at first, the truth is that they are not as hard as they look—if you know the Latin stems. The word *subterranean*, for example, is only a combination of **sub**, under, and **terr**, land. A cave, in other words, is subterranean, because it is underground!

So most of what we call big words or hard words are really not so difficult after all, if you know the Latin stems that are in them.

Each time you learn one easy stem, you have learned an important part of dozens of English words; so learning Latin stems is *power-learning*, because you only have to study one small thing in order to learn part of dozens of things!

In this book, you are going to learn lots of Latin (and even a few Greek) stems. As you learn more and more, you will begin to notice them everywhere you go. You will find Latin stems in the words of newspapers, books, and news programs. You will hear educated adults use words that have Latin stems. You will sometimes hear a word for the very first time, but you will know what it means anyway, because you know all of the Latin stems in it.

You now see why this book is part of a series of books called *The Word Within the Word*—because our modern English words have these ancient Latin words inside them. There are ancient words inside our modern words.

And we are going to find out what they are.

A second feature of this book is a series of words that are prominent in the great books of American and British literature. These classic words are almost all of Latin origin (we have included a few from other sources), which is yet another indication of the powerful importance of Latin to the modern English language. In chapters that feature these great Latin-based words, you will see that they have been used by famous writers of English literature for many centuries, and have formed a central core of advanced literary language. The words you will learn are so central that you will find them again and again, in almost every good book you ever read.

The definitions you will learn of these classic English words are only a beginning. When you learn the word *exquisite*, and the definition we use here (beautifully made), it is important to realize that like most words *exquisite* has other related meanings; it can also mean intricate, delicate, flawless and other similar things. Think flexibly.

All of the quizzes in this book are cumulative. In other words, the quiz on lesson four is really on lessons one through four; you must prepare yourself to be a proud, disciplined student, reviewing all lists for all quizzes. The point is to learn these stems and words now, and to know them for the rest of your life. That is a good idea, because they are of such high quality that you will always need them.

We have taken pains in this book to frame this vocabulary study in its true light, the light of a vanished, Roman culture. You will see images from Rome, read quotations from Roman philosophers, and read Roman facts. Always remember that this is not just an imaginary fiction; the language you speak and think with is truly a collection of echoes from the ancient past, from Caesar's world.

Have fun.

Grammar Review

In *Caesar's English*, the use of words is explained in the language of grammar. To be specific, most words are discussed in terms of their parts of speech. The parts of speech are the eight kinds of words in English. Did you realize that there are only eight kinds of words?

The eight parts of speech (kinds of words) in English are:

NOUN - the name of a person, place or thing.
PRONOUN - a word that takes the place of a noun.
ADJECTIVE - a word that modifies a noun or a pronoun.

VERB - a word that shows action, being, or links a subject to another word. Jumped, is.
ADVERB - a word that modifies a verb, adjective, or another adverb.

PREPOSITION - a word that shows the relationship between its object and another word in the sentence.
CONJUNCTION - a word that joins two words or two groups of words.
INTERJECTION - a word that shows emotion but has no grammatical function.

Examples:

Yes, he suddenly saw the tall Roman and the short Gaul.
interj. pron. adv. v. adj. adj. n. conj. adj. adj. n.

Caesar's English
Ancient Latin Stems
Lesson One

Latin Stems

stem	meaning	modern examples
bi	(two)	bicycle, biped, bilateral
sub	(under)	submarine, submerge, subtract
de	(down)	descend, deposit, deduce
pre	(before)	predict, prepare, prelude
super	(over)	supervise, superior, superb

Latin Stem Talk

BI means two. A *bicycle* has two wheels, a *biped* (like you) has two feet, *bilateral* means two-sided, and a *bimonthly* magazine comes out every two months!

SUB means under. A *submarine* goes under the sea, to *submerge* is to pull something under the surface, and to *subtract* is a kind of arithmetic where you take away (pull under) one number from another!

DE means down. To *descend* is to go down, to *deposit* is to put down, to *deduce* is to think your way down from a big truth.

PRE means before. To *predict* is to announce something before it even happens; to *prepare* is to get ready before an event; a *preschool* is an early school before first grade, and a *prelude* is the music before a performance.

SUPER means over. To *supervise* is to watch over people; a *superman* is someone with powers over and above the norm; *superior* means over others in quality, and so does *superb*. Notice that **super** and **sub** are opposites!

Caesar's Analogy

An analogy is a relationship in which the relationships in pairs of things resemble each other. For example, a **giant** is **tall** as a **mountain** is **high**. In each case, the adjective describes the height of the noun. We could express the analogy this way, as a multiple choice guessing game:

TALL : GIANT ::
    a. tire : car
    b. window : house
    c. high : mountain
    d. red : sunset

Notice that only one of the four answers is best: high/mountain. Red is not the height of the sunset; it is the color of it. Tire is not the height of a car; it is a part of it. Sometimes a relationship is like **tall** and **giant**; one word is a characteristic of the other. Sometimes the relationship is of opposites: **up** is to **down** as **full** is to **empty**. Sometimes the relationship is of part and whole: **dial** is to **radio** as **handle** is to **drawer**. Sometimes the relationship is of synonyms: **dark** is to **obscure** as **bright** is to **luminous**. There can be many different kinds of relationships, but we are looking for a second pair that have the same relationship to each other as the first pair has.

Sometimes it really helps to put the relationship into a sentence, so that you can get the meaning. For example, for the terms *student* and *class*, you could say "The student is **a member of** the class." That way, if you saw the terms *musician* and *band*, you could say "The musician is **a member of** the band" and you would be able to see the same relationship.

It is important to realize that the relationship in the second pair must be in the same direction, order, or sequence as the relationship in the first pair. For example, if we use the part-to-whole relationship, we might have *chimney* is a part of a *house* as fender is a part of a car. So **chimney : house :: fender : car** works. But if it were switched to **chimney : house :: car : fender**, it would be false. See if you can solve the following analogy:

DESCEND : ASCEND ::
   a. bicycle : tricycle
   b. submerge : emerge
   c. man : superman
   d. school : preschool

Advanced Word: Superfluous

From the Latin *superfluus*, the English adjective **superfluous** (soo-PURR-flew-us; stress the second syllable, not the third) contains the stems **super** (over) and **flu** (flow). It means overflowing, excessive, lots and lots, too much. **Superfluous** is an adjective; it can modify either a noun or a pronoun, so you could have superfluous wealth or superfluous curls on your head. A foolish person will sometimes make superfluous comments: the talker has made all the comments that can be endured, and now the superfluous comments begin to over-flow! I hope this explanation was not superfluous. More on this word later.

Who's That Writer?

James M. Barrie, the author of *Peter Pan*, was born in Kirriemuir, Scotland, in 1860. He wrote plays and novels, and viewed life as a great adventure. He wrote *Peter Pan* in 1904 when he was living in London. The classic story of Never Never Land stressed the theme of childlike innocence. Barrie died in 1937.

Caesar's Spanish

stem	meaning	English / Spanish examples
bi	(two)	bicycle / bicicleta
sub	(under)	submarine / submarino
de	(down)	deposit / depositar
pre	(before)	predict / predecir
super	(over)	supersonic / supersónico

Look closely at each pair of cognates (words that are relatives in each language), and notice that English and Spanish both descend from ancient Roman Latin. By the time you finish this book, you will see that many Spanish words are almost the same as English words, and this is because they are made from the same thing: an ancient Roman word. This makes Spanish a very good language to learn.

JUNO

A Roman Fact

When the Roman emperor Vespasian was shown a hoisting machine that would reduce the need for workmen in construction, he refused to use the machine. He explained, "I must feed my poor."

Julius Caesar, from his *Commentaries on the Gallic Wars*:

Gaul consists of three areas, inhabited by the Belgae, the Aquitani, and people who call themselves Celts, though we call them the Gauls. These people all have different languages, customs, and laws.

VESPASIAN

Caesar's Word Search

In the box below, find the Latin-based English words. They might be vertical, horizontal, or at angles. Circle each word that you find.

```
P R E L U D E P Q Z S P B G
P F B W O C D R Y B T B F N
J R B I P E D E Z F C N R S
S S S P B D E D P T Z P L U
U U U T I E B I R O N Q P B
P B P L L D I C U Z S E O M
E M E N A U C T U P S I G E
R A R N T C Y J N I Y D T R
B R I L E E C J V A K X G G
I I O M R N L R M G U P G E
G N R P A B E N U W E J J Q
U E F Y L P D E S C E N D Z
A X Q S U B T R A C T K P O
A D Z S D S P R E P A R E V
```

_ BICYCLE   _ SUBMARINE   _ DESCEND   _ PREDICT
_ SUPERVISE   _ BIPED   _ SUBMERGE   _ DEPOSIT
_ PREPARE   _ SUPERIOR   _ BILATERAL   _ SUBTRACT
_ DEDUCE   _ PRELUDE   _ SUPERB

Real Latin

Filius patris simillus.
The son is exactly like his father.

Many a time,...
from a
bad beginning
great friendships
have sprung up.

- Terence
185-159 B.C.

Caesar's English
Vocabulary from Latin
Lesson Two

1. **countenance**: facial expression
2. **profound**: deep
3. **manifest**: obvious
4. **prodigious**: huge
5. **languor**: weakness

countenance

The English noun **countenance** refers to the contents of the face. A person's countenance can be cheerful, stormy, or melancholy. You might see a smiling countenance or a morose (sad and gloomy) countenance. There could be a look of disappointment on the countenance. James M. Barrie wrote, in *Peter Pan*, that "This ill-luck had given a gentle melancholy to his countenance." In Robert Louis Stevenson's book *Dr. Jekyll and Mr. Hyde*, there is a man of "rugged countenance that was never lighted by a smile" and a "grave countenance." James Fennimore Cooper used **countenance** in his 1826 novel *The Last of the Mohicans*: "The countenance of Hawk-eye was haggard and careworn, and his air dejected." In *Tom Sawyer*, Mark Twain wrote that "A boding uneasiness took possession of every countenance."

Countenance is a very old English word. Coming from the Latin *continentia*, it was even used by Geoffrey Chaucer in his 1385 poem, *The Canterbury Tales*, to describe one who is enduring woe (sadness), but who does not let heaviness show on his countenance; Chaucer wrote, "As I may best, I wol my wo endure, ne make no contenance of hevinesse." As you can see, English spelling has changed a lot in 600 years!

What do you think Charles Dickens meant by "the florid countenance of Mr. Stryver"?

profound

The adjective **profound**, from the Latin *profundus*, means deep, and in a related way, it can also mean complete or even absolute. An ocean can be profound, but so can an idea, as in profound philosophy. There can be profound differences between people. Richard Wright wrote about a profound silence. In James M. Barrie's *Peter Pan*, Captain Hook was "profoundly dejected," which meant that he was deeply sad. Sylvia Plath described "the profound void of an empty stomach," and in *The Double Helix*, James Watson described "the heart of a profound insight into the nature of life itself." In *Why We Can't Wait*, Martin Luther King wrote, "What silenced me was a profound sense of awe." In *Hamlet*, Shakespeare described Hamlet's odd behavior this way: "He raised a sigh so piteous and profound as it did seem to shatter all his bulk and end his being."

Could a countenance be profound?

What do you think Jonathan Swift meant in his 1726 book, *Gulliver's Travels*, when he described "profound learning"? In what way can learning be profound?

manifest

The English adjective **manifest** comes from the Latin *manifestus* and means obvious. When something is manifest, it is completely apparent and open to view. The noun form of this word is **manifestation**, and there is even a verb form: something can **manifest** itself, meaning make itself obvious or clear. In George Orwell's 1945 book *Animal Farm*, he wrote that the pigs were "manifestly cleverer than the other animals." In his great American classic *Walden*, Henry David Thoreau wrote that "The squirrels manifest no concern whether the woods will bear chestnuts this year or not." And Martin Luther King wrote that "The yearning for freedom eventually manifests itself."

Could confidence be manifest on your countenance?

What did Jack London mean when he wrote in *The Call of the Wild* that "To Buck's surprise these dogs manifested no jealousy toward him"?

prodigious

The English adjective **prodigious**, from the Latin *prodigiosus*, means huge or marvelous. Things that are prodigious are amazing. Rachel Carson wrote in *Silent Spring* that in the wild, microscopic mites and other insects are present in "prodigious numbers." *Silent Spring* was a science book that helped warn the world of the dangers of DDT and other toxic pesticides. In *The Yearling*, Marjorie Kinnan Rawlings wrote that "The effort needed to move the dead weight was prodigious." In his play *The Crucible*, Arthur Miller wrote, "There is a prodigious stench in this place." Robert Louis Stevenson wrote about prodigious numbers of seagulls and of a "prodigious valley, strewn with rocks and where ran a foaming river."

Exactly what did Stevenson mean in *Treasure Island* when he wrote, "The Spaniards were so prodigiously afraid of him."

languor

Languor is weakness, either of body or of mind. Languor comes from the Latin verb *languere*, to languish. If you are weak, weary, tired, or droopy, you are in a state of languor. The noun **languor** can transform and appear as the adjectives **languid** and **languorous** or as the verb **languish**. When we feel languor, our gestures and movements can be languid or languorous, such as the weak wave of the hand we make when we are tired. We can also speak in a tired, weak, languid way. The Irish writer James Joyce once wrote that "A languorous weariness passed over him." If it gets very hot, we might feel languid; in *The Secret Garden*, Frances Hodgson Burnett wrote, "In India she had always felt hot and too languid to care much about anything." In Grahame's *The Wind in the Willows*, the lazy Toad replies languidly. We can even describe things in nature this way: Joseph Conrad refers to the "oily and languid sea" in his novel *Heart of Darkness*. One of the best sentences comes from H.G. Wells, who described a Martian invasion in his novel, *The War of the Worlds*. We never learn the name of the main character who narrates the book, but at one point he says, "My movements were languid, my plans of the vaguest."

Could it be manifest that you were profoundly languorous? Could you have a languid countenance?

Who's That Writer?

Marjorie Kinnan Rawlings, the author of *The Yearling*, was born in Washington, D.C., in 1896. She began writing when she was six years old, and earned a degree in English from the University of Wisconsin. Rawlings fell in love with Florida during a visit to her brother-in-law in 1926, and returned in 1928 to buy seventy-two acres at Cross Creek, near Gainesville. In 1939 *The Yearling* won the Pulitzer Prize. Rawlings died in 1953 at the age of fifty-seven.

What is This Writer Saying?

Discuss the meaning of the bold word in each of the following sentences:

From George Orwell's *Animal Farm*: "Napoleon appeared to change **countenance**."

From James M. Barrie's *Peter Pan*: "His eyes were of the blue of the forget-me-not, and of a **profound** melancholy."

From James Watson's *The Double Helix*: "The combination of his **prodigious** mind and his infectious grin was unbeatable."

From Rachel Carson's *Silent Spring*: "Toxins may sleep long in the body, to become **manifest** months or years later in an obscure disorder almost impossible to trace to its origins."

From Frederick Douglass's *The Narrative of Frederick Douglass*: "My natural elasticity was crushed, my intellect **languished**, the disposition to read departed."

Caesar's Spanish

Everywhere we turn, language reveals to us that modern English and modern Spanish are both descendants of ancient Latin:

Latin	*Spanish*	*English*
profundus	profundo	profound
manifestus	manifesto	manifest
prodigiosus	prodigioso	prodigious
languidus	lánguido	languid

Caesar's Synonyms

Here are words that are similar to the words in our list, but are they exactly the same in meaning? Or are they slightly different? For each word on our list, look up any synonym that you do not know, then pick one, and carefully explain the difference between it and our word.

countenance: visage, expression, physiognomy, look, aspect, presence, mien, air, lineament, appearance

profound: deep, far-reaching, absolute, thorough, penetrating, unqualified, enlightened, wise, sapient, sagacious, judicious

manifest: obvious, apparent, illustrate, evince, typify, embody, personify, distinct, conspicuous, evident, noticeable, observable, palpable, unmistakable, plain

prodigious: great, enormous, marvelous, extraordinary, large, powerful, vast

languor: dreaminess, laziness, listlessness, quiet, stillness, inertia, lassitude, inaction, idleness, dormancy, stupor, torpidity, sluggishness, stagnation, drowsiness, somnolence

Caesar's Rewrites

Here are some sentences from famous books. In each case, rewrite the sentence into more ordinary words. Example from Marjorie Rawlings's *The Yearling*: "A languor crept over him." The rewrite: Little by little, he began to feel lazy.

From James Barrie's *Peter Pan*: "This ill-luck had given a gentle melancholy to his **countenance**."

From Jack London's *Call of the Wild*: "To Buck's surprise these dogs **manifested** no jealousy toward him."

From Frances Hodgson Burnett's *The Secret Garden*: "In India she had always felt hot and too **languid** to care much about anything."

From Mark Twain's *Tom Sawyer*: "The middle-aged man turned out to be a **prodigious** personage—no less than the county judge."

From Ralph Ellison's *Invisible Man*: "I felt **profoundly** sad, as though winter had fallen during the hour."

Real Latin

Vestis virum facit.
Clothes make the man.

Caesar's Antonyms

For each of the words in this lesson, think of a word that means the opposite. A word that means the opposite is known as an *antonym*.

1. **countenance**
2. **profound**
3. **manifest**
4. **prodigious**
5. **languor**

Are there any words in this list that have no antonyms? Are there any that it is very difficult to think of an antonym for? Why?

Caesar's Analogies

Analogies are about relationships. Find a second pair of words that have the same relationship to each other as the first pair has. Remember that it sometimes helps to put the two words into a sentence that makes the relationship clear.

MANIFEST : OBSERVABLE ::
a. acute : pain
b. odious : lovable
c. languor : weakness
d. condescend : admire

WISDOM : PROFOUND ::
a. acute : blunt
b. prodigious : microscopic
c. countenance : expression
d. languor : weak

Review for Cumulative Quiz

bi	two
sub	under
de	down
pre	before
super	over
countenance	facial expression
profound	deep
manifest	obvious
prodigious	huge
languor	weakness

countenance
facial expression

Found you
no displeasure
in him
by word
nor countenance?

\- William Shakespeare
King Lear

Caesar's English
Ancient Latin Stems
Lesson Three

Latin Stem List

stem	meaning	examples
un	(not)	unequal, unable, undone
inter	(between)	international, interstellar, interject
semi	(half)	semicircle, semiformal, semiannual
dis	(away)	dismiss, distract, distort
sym	(together)	symphony, sympathy, symmetry

Latin Stem Talk

UN means not. An *undone* task is not completed, an *unprepared* person is not prepared, being *unable* to do something means not being able to do it, and *unequal* bowls of ice cream are not equal!

INTER means between. In the universe, *interstellar* space is the space between the stars. An *international* agreement is an agreement between nations. An *interlude* is a break between two parts of a performance; and to *interject* your opinion into a conversation is to insert yourself between two people who are trying to talk!

SEMI means half. A *semicircle* is a half circle, and a *semiannual* event happens every six months—half a year!

DIS means away. To *dismiss* a class is to send the students away, and to *distract* someone is to draw their attention away!

SYM means together. In a *symphony* orchestra, musicians play together, and when we have *sympathy* for people, we feel a feeling of togetherness with them!

Caesar's Analogy

The first two words are related to each other in a special way. Is one before the other? Is one inside the other? Are they opposites? Find the pair below that has the same relationship as the first pair!

INTERSTELLAR : STARS ::
- a. semicircle : circle
- b. dismiss : convene
- c. air : marbles
- d. unequal : equal

Advanced Word: Symphonic

The word **symphonic** (simm-FONN-ik) contains the Latin stems **sym** (together) and **phon** (sound). Symphonic means harmonic, a condition in which sounds sound good—in harmony—together. **Symphonic** is an adjective; it can modify either a noun or a pronoun, so you could have symphonic music or even symphonic voices. Most big cities have a symphony orchestra, which plays symphonic music, which sounds symphonic to our ears.

Advanced Word: Interpose

The verb **interpose** is a good word. **Interpose** contains the Latin stems **inter**, between, and **pos**, put, and it means to put between, or to interject. People interpose their comments when they interrupt to say something, but we can also interpose an object between other things. For centuries, interpose has been used by great writers, including Milton, Swift, Austen, Cooper, Hawthorne, and Kipling. Jonathan Swift described the "interposition of a cloud" in *Gulliver's Travels*. In *The Last of the Mohicans*, James Fennimore Cooper wrote that it was "as if a supernatural agency had interposed in the behalf of Uncas." Emily Brontë, in her immortal novel *Wuthering Heights*, wrote that "She held her hand interposed between the furnace heat and her eyes." In *Kim*, Kipling wrote that "Father Victor saw Kim edging toward the door, and interposed a strong leg." Frederick Douglass wrote in his autobiography that "Not one interposed a friendly word" and that "In this state I appeared before my master, humbly entreating him to interpose his authority for my protection." In *A Passage to India*, E.M. Forster observed that "The chauffeur interposed aggressively." In 1895 Stephen Crane described a scene from the Civil War in his novel, *The Red Badge of Courage*: "A rolling gray cloud again interposed as the regiment doggedly replied." And William Golding wrote, in his *Lord of the Flies*, that "the vivid phantoms of his day-dream still interposed between him and Piggy."

Which of these examples of **interpose** do you like the best?

How many different meanings of **interpose** do you see?

How many of these novels that use **interpose** have you heard of before?

Who's That Writer?

Emily Brontë, the author of the great romantic novel, *Wuthering Heights*, was born in Thornton, Yorkshire, England, on July 30, 1818. She had one brother and three sisters, including Charlotte, who wrote the great novel *Jane Eyre*. Emily's mother died in 1824. Emily and her sister Charlotte wrote poems and novels when they were children, but when they published *Jane Eyre* and *Wuthering Heights* in 1847, their fame skyrocketed. Emily died in 1848, having caught a cold at her brother's funeral.

Caesar's Spanish

Everywhere we turn, language reveals to us that modern English and modern Spanish are both descendants of ancient Latin:

stem	meaning	English / Spanish examples
un	(not)	unable / incapaz (un = in)
inter	(between)	international / internacional
semi	(half)	semicircle / semicírculo
dis	(away)	distract / distraer
sym	(together)	sympathy / simpatía

A Roman Fact

The emperor Titus (pronounced TIE-tuss) was opposed to capital punishment. During his reign, he executed no one, and even had informers flogged. Once, two patricians (upper class Romans) were caught in a plot to overthrow Titus, and rather than have them executed, he sent them a warning. Then, he sent a messenger to one of the conspirator's worried mothers, assuring her that he would not execute her son.

Caesar's Word Search

In the box below, find the Latin-based English words. They might be vertical, horizontal, or at angles. Circle each word that you find.

```
V H I S S D D Z K Z L T L E
M S Y S E S I O Y X A D U I
A Y I Y M M Y S E P B R N N
B M N M I U I M T N Q H D T
K P T M C N S F P R Y D O E
U A E I A Z A O H A C N R
D T R T R B R K T R O C E S
I H J R C L U E H T M N T T
S Y E Y L E I A Q M X A Y E
M X C T E X Y Q G E R N L L
I N T E R N A T I O N A L L
S J J M L U N E Q U A L O A
S U S I I D I S T O R T J R
S E M I A N N U A L Z J A K
```

__ UNEQUAL   __ INTERNATIONAL   __ SEMICIRCLE   __ DISMISS
__ SYMPHONY   __ UNABLE   __ INTERSTELLAR   __ SEMIFORMAL
__ DISTRACT   __ SYMPATHY   __ UNDONE   __ INTERJECT
__ SEMIANNUAL   __ DISTORT   __ SYMMETRY

Real Latin

Multa dubito.
I have many doubts.

Julius Caesar, from his *Commentaries on the Gallic Wars*:

Caesar hurried preparations for an expedition to Britain, for he knew that in all the Gallic campaigns the Gauls had gotten reinforcements from the Britons. Even if there was not time for a campaign that season, he thought it would be an advantage just to visit the island, to see what its inhabitants were like, and to become acquainted with the land, the harbours, and the landing places. Of all this the Gauls knew nothing.

Review for Cumulative Quiz

bi	two
sub	under
de	down
pre	before
super	over
un	not
inter	between
semi	half
dis	away
sym	together
countenance	facial expression
profound	deep
manifest	obvious
prodigious	huge
languor	weakness

When a building is about to fall down, all the mice desert it.

- Pliny the Elder
23-79 A.D.

Caesar's English
Vocabulary from Latin
Lesson Four

1. **serene**: calm
2. **acute**: sharp
3. **grotesque**: distorted
4. **condescend**: to patronize
5. **odious**: hateful

serene

The adjective **serene** means calm, clear, peaceful. **Serene** comes to English from the Latin *serenus*, which came to Latin from the ancient Greek *xeros*, which meant dry. When a sky is dry, it has no clouds, rain, or storms in it; it is clear and peaceful. Kenneth Grahame, in *The Wind in the Willows*, described "the moon, serene and detached in a cloudless sky." A person's face can be like a peaceful, cloudless sky, too, as when Thomas Hardy wrote of his character's "serene Minerva-eyes" in *The Mayor of Casterbridge*. When we are deeply at peace in our hearts, this internal calm can be called **serene**; Henry David Thoreau, the American thinker who wrote *Walden* about his experiences in the woods, said that "My serenity is rippled but not ruffled." Mary Shelley used **serene** in her novel, *Frankenstein*; she wrote that "A serene sky and verdant fields filled me with ecstasy." Curiously, Shelley also described "serene joy," although the two words seem to suggest very different things. In Jane Austen's novel *Pride and Prejudice*, we read about "the serenity of your sister's countenance."

What would a serene countenance look like? How would it be like a serene sky, or a serene sea? Could you feel profoundly serene?

acute

The English adjective **acute,** meaning sharp, can be traced all the way back to the ancient Romans, where *acus* meant needle in Latin. In mathematics, an acute angle is one that is less than 90 degrees. When someone has a sharp mind, we call that acute, too; in Jonathan Swift's story, *Gulliver's Travels*, someone has a "most acute judgment." There is another sharp mind in Harriet Beecher Stowe's *Uncle Tom's Cabin*, where we see "an expression of great acuteness and shrewdness in his face." A sharp pain is acute; Jane Austen wrote that "her head ached acutely" in her novel *Pride and Prejudice*. In *The Yearling*, Marjorie Rawlings wrote that "The gnawing in his stomach was an acute pain." Having a sense of justice is another kind of acute pain; in *Vanity Fair*, Thackeray asked, "who has a sense of wrong so acute, and so glowing a gratitude for kindness, as a generous boy?"

Do you think someone's mind could be both profound and acute? Could it be acute and serene at the same time?

grotesque

The adjective **grotesque** comes to English from the Italian Renaissance, where workmen who were digging a foundation suddenly had the ground fall away from them, and a great hole opened up. When they peered into the opening, they could see that it was not a natural cavern, but was a ruin; they were staring down into ancient rooms! Soon, they realized that they had discovered the long-buried remains of Roman Emperor Nero's great palace, that later emperors had destroyed. When the artist Raphael heard about the find, he raced across town and had himself lowered down into the hole on a rope. He carried a torch with him, and when he held out the torch, he could see strange, distorted artwork all over the walls: weird animals and twisted human faces, creepy, exaggerated shapes. For the Italians, this weird, distorted style became known by the underground *grotto* where it was found; it was *grotto-esque*, and our word **grotesque** is the result. Interrestingly, the word grotto traces back to the vulgar Latin word crypta, hidden. We use the adjective **grotesque** to describe things that are physically weird looking, such as in novelist John Gardner's *Grendel*, where he describes "grotesquely muscled shoulders." In *The Jungle*, Upton Sinclair wrote that a character "wore green spectacles, that gave him a grotesque appearance." H.G. Wells wrote, in *The War of the Worlds*, that "huge black shapes, grotesque and strange, moved busily to and fro." In Thornton Wilder's novel *The Bridge of San Luis Rey*, he wrote that the "almost grotesque and hungry face became beautiful." And Joseph Conrad wrote that "they had faces like grotesque masks" in his novel *Heart of Darkness*.

We do not always, however, use **grotesque** to describe physical appearances. In *Tom Sawyer*, Mark Twain wrote that "He kept up this grotesque foolishness." In *Uncle Tom's Cabin*, Harriet Beecher Stowe described "one of those wild grotesque songs." And in *Grendel*, John Gardner wrote, "I scream, facing him, grotesquely shaking hands."

In what way is grotesquely shaking hands similar to grotesquely muscled shoulders? How are grotesque masks like grotesque foolishness? What are some other examples of grotesque things that you can think of?

condescend

To **condescend** usually means to act superior to someone else, to act as though you have to descend down to their inferior level, that is lower than your own. The person who condescends might act as though it is unpleasant to converse with you, or as though he or she is doing you a favor to speak, and as though he is pleased with himself for being so generous. In Harper Lee's novel *To Kill A Mockingbird*, the younger sister Scout Finch says that her older brother "Jem condescended to take me to school the first day." In *Peter Pan*, Barrie writes that "he would answer condescendingly." In Stephen Crane's masterpiece, *The Red Badge of Courage*, about a young boy named Henry Fleming who goes to fight in the Civil War, Henry "reflected, with condescending pity: 'Too bad! Too bad! The poor devil, it makes him feel tough!'" In Emily Brontë's classic *Wuthering Heights*, "She was forced to condescend to our company." In Mark Twain's *Tom Sawyer*, "These two great commanders did not condescend to fight in person."

Sometimes, **condescend** has a different meaning, which is not so offensive to our feelings. It can refer to a situation where someone in authority or high rank sincerely does something considerate for someone else, perhaps for someone who is poor or helpless, and who may appreciate the effort. In Charlotte Brontë's *Jane Eyre*, Jane says, "I did not feel insensible to his condescension, and would not seem so."

Interestingly, **condescend** is one of the oldest words in the English language. From the Latin *condescendere*, it was even used in 1385 by Geoffrey Chaucer in his great poem *The Canterbury Tales*, and in 1667 by Milton, who wrote in *Paradise Lost*, "Gentle to me and affable hath been / Thy condescension."

What do you think Thackeray meant in *Vanity Fair* when he wrote that "even great English lords and ladies condescended to speak to persons whom they did not know"?

Could someone condescend serenely? What would that mean?

odious

The adjective **odious**, from the Latin *odiosus*, refers to something that is repulsive, repugnant, hateful. We are disgusted by odious things, that can be odious in appearance, in sentiment, or in many other ways. In Robert Louis Stevenson's *Dr. Jekyll and Mr. Hyde*, we read that "A flash of odious joy appeared upon the woman's face." Henry

James gave the word a twist in his novel *The American*, writing, "You have been odiously successful." In *The House of the Seven Gables*, Nathaniel Hawthorne wrote, " Why do you keep that odious picture on the wall?" In Jane Austen's *Pride and Prejudice*, we read, "Pray do not talk to that odious man."

Could someone have an odious expression on his or her face? Is it odious to condescend? Could something be odious and grotesque at the same time? Could something be profoundly odious?

Who's That Writer?

Kenneth Grahame, the author of *The Wind in the Willows*, was born in Edinburgh, Scotland, in 1859, just before the American Civil War. Grahame was educated at St. Edward's School, Oxford, and began professional life at the Bank of England. He began writing fiction in his spare time, and originally wrote chapters of *The Wind in the Willows* as letters to his son, Alistair. When *The Wind in the Willows* was published, it earned Grahame an international reputation. He followed with two sequels, *Toad Triumphant* and *The Willows and Beyond*. Grahame died on July 6, 1932.

What Is This Writer Saying?

Discuss the meaning of the bold word in each of the following sentences:

> From Scott Fitzgerald's *The Great Gatsby*: "I see it as a night scene by El Greco: a hundred houses, at once conventional and **grotesque**, crouching under a sullen, overhanging sky and a lusterless moon."

> From Mark Twain's *Tom Sawyer:* "...heard the stony hearted liar reel off his **serene** statement."

From Frances Hodgson Burnett's *The Secret Garden*: "The Rajah **condescended** to seat himself on a rug under a tree."

From Mark Twain's *Tom Sawyer*: "It made the going into captivity and fetters again so much more **odious**."

From Jean Craighead George's *Julie of the Wolves*: "He turned his head almost upside down to get a more **acute** focus on her."

Caesar's Synonyms

Here are words that are similar to the words in our list, but are they exactly the same in meaning? Or are they slightly different? For each word on our list, look up any synonym that you do not know, then pick one, and carefully explain the difference between it and our word.

serene: unclouded, bright, tranquil, placid, peaceful, quiet, still, unruffled, even, calm, asleep

acute: sharp, sensitive, perceptive, crucial, severe, intense, shrill, keen, penetrating, pointed, peaked, agonizing, fierce, knifelike, piercing

grotesque: distorted, ludicrous, macabre, incongruous, grisly, brutish, outlandish, monstrous, odious, nightmarish, ghastly, hideous, scary, bizarre, dreadful, shocking, fanciful

condescend: patronize, stoop, lower oneself, deign, descend, talk down to, sink to a level below one's dignity

odious: hateful, abhorrent, repugnant, loathsome, detestable, disgusting, repulsive, appalling, deplorable, atrocious, abominable

Real Latin
From Julius Caesar:

Gallia est omnis divisa in partes tres.
All of Gaul is divided into three parts.

Caesar's Analogies
Analogies are about relationships. Find a second pair of words that have the same relationship to each other as the first pair has. Remember that it sometimes helps to put the two words into a sentence that makes the relationship clear.

SERENE : AGITATED ::
    a. loud : quiet
    b. profound : deep
    c. odious : mask
    d. countenance : strange

Caesar's Spanish
Everywhere we turn, language reveals to us that modern English and modern Spanish are both descendants of ancient Latin:

Latin	Spanish	English
acutus	agudo	acute
serenus	sereno	serene
condescendere	condescender	condescend
odiosus	odioso	odious

A Wordy Story...

On a serene spring afternoon, under a prodigious blue sky, an odious elf crept through the growing grass, a condescending sneer of profound arrogance acutely manifest on his sneering countenance. With a grotesque chuckle that disturbed the languorous day, he suddenly stopped, and hopped away, vanishing into the deep shadows of the trees that bordered the field.

Caesar's Rewrites

Here are some sentences from famous books. In each case, rewrite the sentence into more ordinary words. Example from Marjorie Rawlings's *The Yearling*: "A languor crept over him." The rewrite: Little by little, he began to feel lazy.

From Jane Austen's *Pride and Prejudice*: "Her head ached **acutely**."

From Mary Shelley's *Frankenstein*: "He looks upon study as an **odious** fetter."

From Emily Brontë's *Wuthering Heights*: "She was forced to **condescend** to our company."

From H.G. Wells's *The War of the Worlds*: "The Martian, without using his Heat-Ray, walked **serenely** over their guns."

From Harriet Beecher Stowe's *Uncle Tom's Cabin*: "He could cut cunning little baskets out of cherry stones, could make **grotesque** faces on hickory nuts."

Caesar's Favorite Word

Think carefully about each of the words in this lesson—**serene**, **acute**, **grotesque**, **condescend**, and **odious**—and predict which of this lesson's words you will use most often. Explain why you made this word your choice, and give at least three examples of situations in which you could use that word.

Caesar's Antonyms

For each of the words in this lesson, think of a word that means the opposite. A word that means the opposite is known as an *antonym*.

1.   **serene**
2.   **acute**
3.   **grotesque**
4.   **condescend**
5.   **odious**

Are there any words in this list that have no antonyms? Are there any that it is very difficult to think of an antonym for? Why?

Review for Cumulative Quiz

bi	two
sub	under
de	down
pre	before
super	over
un	not
inter	between
semi	half
dis	away
sym	together
countenance	facial expression
profound	deep
manifest	obvious
prodigious	huge
languor	weakness
serene	calm
acute	sharp
grotesque	distorted
condescend	to patronize
odious	hateful

grotesque

weird, distorted

Great shapes like
big machines rose
out of the dimness, and cast
grotesque black shadows.

-H.G. Wells
The Time Machine

41

Caesar's English
Ancient Latin Stems
Lesson Five

Latin Stem List

stem	meaning	modern examples
circum	(around)	circumnavigate, circumspect, circumvent
mal	(bad)	malevolent, malady, malicious
post	(after)	posthumous, postscript, posterity
equi	(equal)	equilateral, equivocate, equilibrium
ante	(before)	antebellum, antecedent, anterior

Latin Stem Talk

CIRCUM means around. A ship can *circumnavigate* the Earth by sailing around it, to be *circumspect* is to be cautious and looking around, and to *circumvent* the rules is to get around them!

MAL means bad. A *malevolent* person has bad will or evil intentions, a *malady* is when you feel bad, and a *malicious* act is intentionally bad!

POST means after. A *posthumous* award is one given after its recipient has died, a *postscript* is the PS we put at the bottom of a letter after we have written it, and our *posterity* are our descendents who come after us.

EQUI means equal. An *equilateral* triangle has three equal sides, to *equivocate* is to equally take both sides of an issue, and *equlibrium* is a system in balance.

ANTE means before. The *antebellum* period is before the war, the *antecedent* is the noun that comes before the pronoun, and the *anterior* is the front part of something!

Caesar's Analogy

The first two words are related to each other in a special way. Is one before the other? Is one inside the other? Are they opposites? Find the pair below that has the same relationship as the first pair!

CIRCUMNAVIGATE : SHIP ::
  a. postscript : letter
  b. antebellum : war
  c. orbit : satellite
  d. equivocate: speaker

Advanced Word: Circumspect

The word **circumspect** (SIR-come-spect) contains the Latin stems **circum** (around) and **spect** (look). It means cautious, careful, on the lookout. **Circumspect** is an adjective, and so it can modify a noun or pronoun. You can have a circumspect spy, a circumspect answer, or a circumspect glance. In order to modify a pronoun, we would have to say something like, "She is circumspect." **Circumspect** is like a one-word poem (I call them *micropoems*) because it has a little visual image of the careful person looking (spect) around (circum)!

Advanced Word: Malevolence

The noun **malevolence** is creepy! **Malevolence** means being mean, having bad (mal) will (vol) toward someone. **Malevolence** is the opposite of **benevolence**, which means kindness, and it can transform into the adjective **malevolent**. **Malevolence** was used nearly 400 years ago by Shakespeare in his play *Macbeth* to describe "the malevolence of fortune." It was also used by Sir Walter Scott in *Ivanhoe* to describe a "wrathful malevolence" and to describe "any avaricious or malevolent noble." (The word *avaricious* means greedy.) Charlotte Brontë referred to "malevolent scorn" in her novel *Jane Eyre*. **Malevolence** has also been used by Charles Dickens, by Joseph Conrad, and by William Golding, who used the adverb form in *Lord of the Flies*: "He looked malevolently at Jack." One of the best sentences comes from Harper Lee, who wrote, in *To Kill A Mockingbird*, that "Inside the house lived a malevolent phantom."

Which of these examples of **malevolence** do you like the best?

How many different meanings of **malevolence** do you see?

How many of these novels that use **malevolence** have you heard of before?

Who's That Writer?

Sir Walter Scott was born in Edinburgh, Scotland, on August 15, 1771. He was trained as a lawyer and became a legal official, a profession that gave him time to write. Scott loved ballads and legends, and wrote a great deal of poetry in his early life, but in 1814 he began writing novels, and eventually wrote more than twenty novels. With the profits from his novels, he built a great mansion in Abbotsford and was named a baronet. Scott was the first great historical novelist, and he influenced later writers such as James Fennimore Cooper, Honoré de Balzac, Charles Dickens, and William Makepeace Thackeray. Scott's 1819 classic *Ivanhoe* is one of the great adventures of knights in all of English literature. It is particularly notable for its descriptions of how the Norman French conquered Anglo Saxon England, and for its modern female characters. Together with the poet Robert Burns, Scott helped to create Scottish literature.

Caesar's Spanish

A study of their stems shows that English and Spanish are related languages, using the same stems to make similar words.

stem	meaning	English / Spanish examples
circum	(around)	circumspect / circunspecto
mal	(bad)	malevolent / malévolo
post	(after)	posthumous / póstumo
equi	(equal)	equilateral / equilátero
ante	(before)	antecedent / antecedente

In these pairs of cognates, we continue to see the wonderful similarity between English words and Spanish words. In fact, each of these words features two stems in a row, and in every case the Spanish word uses the same two Latin stems that the English word uses:

circum around, **spect** look
mal bad, **vol** will
post after, **hum** earth
equi equal, **lat** side
ante before, **cede** go

Clearly, English and Spanish are sibling languages.

Roman Fact

The Roman emperor Trajan provided one of the most important principles of American law. He said, "It is better that the guilty should remain unpunished than that the innocent should be condemned." This helps to explain why our legal systems defines us as "innocent until proven guilty." This principle is also sometimes called the "presumption of innocence."

Caesar's Word Search

In the box below, find the Latin-based English words. They might be vertical, horizontal, or at angles. Circle each word that you find.

```
K E E Q U I L I B R I U M M
H D Q P O S T H U M O U S A
P C P O S T S C R I P T V L
O A I V N I I M A L A D Y I
S A B R A A N T E R I O R C
T B T P C K S E H M E J E I
E C I R C U M S P E C T V O
R G B T R R M Q T L X W Z U
I M C E Q U I V O C A T E S
T E Q U I L A T E R A L Y H
Y A N T E C E D E N T N K D
A N T E B E L L U M T V Q P
A C I R C U M S C R I B E O
O M A L E V O L E N T A F G
```

__ CIRCUMSCRIBE	__ CIRCUMSPECT	__ CIRCUMVENT	__ MALEVOLENT
__ MALADY	__ MALICIOUS	__ POSTHUMOUS	__ POSTSCRIPT
__ POSTERITY	__ EQUILATERAL	__ EQUIVOCATE	__ EQUILIBRIUM
__ ANTEBELLUM	__ ANTECEDENT	__ ANTERIOR	

Real Latin

Pudet me tui.
I am ashamed of us.

Review for Cumulative Quiz

bi	two
sub	under
de	down
pre	before
super	over
un	not
inter	between
semi	half
dis	away
sym	together
circum	around
mal	bad
post	after
equi	equal
ante	before
countenance	facial expression
profound	deep
manifest	obvious
prodigious	huge
languor	weakness
serene	calm
acute	sharp
grotesque	distorted
condescend	to patronize
odious	hateful

It is certain because it is impossible.

- Tertullian
160-240 A.D.

Caesar's English
Vocabulary from Latin
Lesson Six

1. **exquisite**: beautifully made
2. **clamor**: outcry
3. **sublime**: lofty
4. **tremulous**: quivering
5. **allude**: indirectly refer to

exquisite

The English adjective **exquisite** (and its adverb form **exquisitely**) comes to us from the Romans. In Latin, *exquisitus* was a form of *exquirere*, to search out. When we say that something is exquisite, meaning that it is delicately beautiful, or that it is exceptionally perfect, we are echoing the old Roman idea that an exquisite thing is something you don't see every day; it is something rare that you might search a long time to find. In literature, we find **exquisite** used to modify a surprising range of nouns: there are exquisite echoes, exquisite daughters, and exquisite dishes. There are exquisite manners. In James M. Barrie's novel *Peter Pan*, we read, "It was a girl called Tinker Bell exquisitely gowned in a skeleton leaf." In Joseph Conrad's *Lord Jim* a butterfly spreads out dark bronze wings "with exquisite white veinings." In Stephen Crane's *The Red Badge of Courage* the young soldier relaxes because "An exquisite drowsiness had spread through him." Most of the time, **exquisite** refers to things that are good, but sometimes it describes a bad thing that is extremely unusual, as when Jack London wrote in *The Call of the Wild* that "All the pain he had endured was as nothing compared with the exquisite agony of this." In Robert Louis Stevenson's *Dr. Jekyll and Mr. Hyde*, we read with a chill that "my blood was changed into something exquisitely thin and icy." What do you think Rachel Carson meant by her use of **exquisite** in *Silent Spring* when she wrote, "These include three of the thrushes whose songs are among the most exquisite of bird voices..."?

clamor

The English noun **clamor** comes from the Latin *clamor*, and the Latin verb *clamare*, to cry out. **Clamor** is sometimes spelled **clamour**. A clamor is no mild call; it is a loud outcry, a vociferous uproar, and especially one that continues on, vehemently. People *keep* clamoring. **Clamor** is a strong word; it should not be wasted on any old holler. In English and American literature we find **clamor** used by William Golding, George Orwell, and Richard Wright. We find it used by modern writers like Eudora Welty, and by Geoffrey Chaucer in 1385: "He maketh that the grete tour resoundeth of his youling and clamour." Notice the very old spellings of Chaucer's words. In *Macbeth*, Shakespeare wrote that "the obscure bird clamoured the livelong night." The obscure bird, apparently, was an owl. In Walter Scott's 1820 novel *Ivanhoe*, we read about "the clamorous yells and barking of all the dogs in the hall." In *Tom Sawyer* Mark Twain wrote about the "glad clamor of laughter." One of the most creative uses of **clamor** comes from *The Call of the Wild*, where Jack London wrote that "He did not steal for joy of it, but because of the clamour of his stomach."

sublime

If the English adjective **sublime** means noble or majestic (and it does, it does), then why does it contain the Latin stem *sub* that means under? Well, in Rome, honored objects were placed up on or under (*sub*) the mantel (*limen*), where they could be seen, and so **sublime** means not down, but up, up under the mantel: up *sub* the *limen*. As many words do, **sublime** has a number of possible meanings, but they all connote a high, lofty state. **Sublime** may mean exalted, or inspiring, or grand. It may mean outstanding or supreme. Sometimes we use the word as a noun, and refer to *the sublime*. Martin Luther King wrote about "sublime courage." Mark Twain wrote about the "sublimity of his language," and Harriet Beecher Stowe wrote about "sublime heroism." In *Gulliver's Travels*, Jonathan Swift wrote of things that could be "comprehended only by a few persons of sublime genius." Stephen Crane described the courage of battle as a "temporary but sublime absence of selfishness." One of the most charming **sublime** sentences comes from Barrie's *Peter Pan*, where "Now we are rewarded for our sublime faith in a mother's love." What does Barrie mean by "sublime faith"?

tremulous

Our English adjective **tremulous** is a direct descendent of the Latin *tremulus* and the verb *tremere*, to tremble. We call tremulous those who are trembling, who are shaking with tremors, or who are overly timid. Tremulous quivering, especially of the hand or voice, might be a result of fear, nervousness, or weakness, and it might have either a physical or psychological origin.

Tremulous has been a popular word among English and American writers for at least three centuries and has been used by Walter Scott, Nathaniel Hawthorne, Lewis Carroll, and Robert Louis Stevenson. Sometimes **tremulous** can describe the quivering of a musical note, as when Ralph Ellison writes of "a tremulous, blue-toned chord." Sometimes **tremulous** describes the trembling of a voice, as when William Golding writes that "Jack's voice went up, tremulous yet determined..." Lewis Carroll also used **tremulous** to describe the human voice in *Alice's Adventures in Wonderland*; Carroll wrote, "His voice has a timid and tremulous sound." Frances Hodgson Burnett used **tremulous** in her novel *The Secret Garden*, where there were "two rabbits sitting up and sniffing with tremulous noses." In *Peter Pan*, "John whispered tremulously." In Robert Louis Stevenson's *Kidnapped*, there was a "rather tremulous laughter." In *Leaves of Grass*, America's great poet Walt Whitman wrote that the "cattle stand and shake away flies with the tremulous shuddering of their hides."

What does it mean in Thackeray's novel *Vanity Fair* when we read, "he opened the letter rather tremulously"?

allude

To allude to something is to make an indirect reference to it, to hint. The English verb **allude** (and its noun form **allusion**) comes to us from Latin, where we learn that the Latin verb *alludere* meant to play with! So **allude** is a word with spirit. Alluding to things, rather than directly stating them, gives us a playful option: we can call someone's attention to something without directly mentioning it. Alluding is a game of hints and guesses. In George Eliot's *Silas Marner* we read that "It was already four years since there had been any allusion to the subject between them." In Mary Shelley's novel *Frankenstein*, a character begs, "But until then, I conjure you, do not mention or allude to it." In his famous novel, *A Passage to India*, E.M. Forster writes, "They attacked one another with obscure allusions and had a silly quarrel." One of the very best sentences comes from Kenneth Grahame's children's classic, *The Wind in the Willows*, where we learn one of the most important differences between animals and people; Grahame writes that "It is quite against animal-etiquette to dwell on possible trouble ahead, or even to allude to it." All of the little animals, we infer, are optimists.

Who's That Writer?

The author of *Alice in Wonderland*, known to us as Lewis Carroll, was really Charles Lutwidge Dodgson. Born in 1832 in Daresbury,

Cheshire, Charles had seven sisters and three brothers. He was first educated at home, and at age seven he was already reading Bunyan's *The Pilgrim's Progress*, a very advanced book indeed. At twelve Dodgson went to private school at Richmond, and in 1845 he went to Rugby School, where his brilliance in mathematics was recognized. After college at Christ Church, Oxford, he accepted a position there as a lecturer in mathematics. In 1856 he published a poem, "Solitude," under the *nom de plume* (pen name) Lewis Carroll. He made friends with the new Oxford dean, Henry Liddell, who had a daughter named Alice. On a picnic, Dodgson told Alice a story in which she was the main character, and she urged him to write it down. He did, offered it to MacMillan publishers under his pen name, and the rest is literary history. Dodgson taught at Christ Church until 1881, published papers in mathematics, and died of pneumonia in 1898.

What is This Writer Saying?

Discuss the meaning of the **bold** word in each of the following sentences:

From Bram Stoker's *Dracula*: "There was no place for words in his **sublime** misery."

From E.M. Forster's *A Passage to India*: "Aziz was **exquisitely** dressed, from tie-pin to spats."

From Richard Wright's *Native Son*: "His feelings **clamored** for an answer his mind could not give."

From James Joyce's *A Portrait of the Artist as a Young Man*: "A **tremulous** chill blew round his heart."

From Thackeray's *Vanity Fair*: "The humble calling of her female parent Miss Sharp never **alluded** to."

Caesar's Synonyms

Here are words that are similar to the words in our list, but are they exactly the same in meaning? Or are they slightly different? For each word on our list, look up any synonym that you do not know, then pick one, and carefully explain the difference between it and our word.

exquisite: dainty, elaborate, graceful, fine, delicate, refined, glamorous, beautiful, intricate

clamor: babel, hubbub, din, uproar, bellow, clatter, blare, pandemonium, yell, racket, bawl, caterwaul, cacophony

sublime: ideal, heavenly, utopian, perfect, idyllic, Arcadian, empyrean, paradisiac, Elysian, Edenic, lofty

tremulous: quivery, trembling, shivering, aquiver, shaky, wobbly, anxious, edgy, frightened, timid, nervous, fearful

allude: mention, comment, touch on, refer to, point out, note, bring up, observe, animadvert, advert, remark

Caesar's Spanish

Everywhere we turn, language reveals to us that modern English and modern Spanish are both descendants of ancient Latin:

Latin	Spanish	English
exquisitus	exquisito	exquisite
clamor	clamor	clamor
sublimis	sublime	sublime
tremulus	trémulo	tremulous
alludere	aludir	allude

Real Latin

From Cicero:

Assiduus usus uni rei deditus et ingenium et artem saepe vincit.

Constant practice devoted to one subject often overcomes both intelligence and skill.

Caesar's Rewrites

Here are some sentences from famous books. In each case, rewrite the sentence into more ordinary words. Example from Marjorie Rawlings's *The Yearling*: "A languor crept over him." The rewrite: Little by little, he began to feel lazy.

From Herman Melville's *Moby Dick*: "For the most part, in this tropic whaling life, a **sublime** uneventfulness invests you; you hear no news; read no gazettes."

From Jack London's *Call of the Wild*: "Every part, brain and body, nerve tissue and fibre, was keyed to the most **exquisite** pitch."

From Kenneth Grahame's *The Wind in the Willows*: "It is quite against animal etiquette to dwell on possible trouble ahead, or even to **allude** to it."

From Robert Louis Stevenson's *Treasure Island*: "But it was rather **tremulous** laughter."

From Richard Wright's *Native Son*: "His feelings **clamored** for an answer his mind could not give."

Caesar's Antonyms

For each of Caesar's English words in this lesson, think of a word that means the opposite. A word that means the opposite is known as an *antonym*.

1. **exquisite**
2. **clamor**
3. **sublime**
4. **tremulous**
5. **allude**

Are there any words in this list that have no antonyms? Are there any that it is very difficult to think of an antonym for? Why?

Caesar's Analogies

Analogies are about relationships. Find a second pair of words that have the same relationship to each other as the first pair has. Remember that it sometimes helps to put the two words into a sentence that makes the relationship clear.

SUBLIME : PEDESTRIAN ::
   a. amiable : peevish
   b. clamor : hubbub
   c. perplex : mystery
   d. clamor : riot

TREMULOUS : FEAR ::
   a. clamorous : anger
   b. incredulous : gullible
   c. sublime : noble
   d. amiable : person

Review for Cumulative Quiz

bi	two
sub	under
de	down
pre	before
super	over
un	not
inter	between
semi	half
dis	away
sym	together
circum	around
mal	bad
post	after
equi	equal
ante	before
countenance	facial expression
profound	deep
manifest	obvious
prodigious	huge
languor	weakness
serene	calm
acute	sharp
grotesque	distorted
condescend	to patronize
odious	hateful
exquisite	beautifully made
clamor	outcry
sublime	lofty
tremulous	quivering
allude	indirectly refer to

exquisite
beautifully made

It was a girl
called Tinkerbell
exquisitely gowned
in a skeleton leaf.

-James M. Barrie
Peter Pan

Caesar's English
Ancient Latin Stems
Lesson Seven

Latin Stem List

stem	meaning	modern examples
aqua	(water)	aquatic, aqueduct, aquarium
audi	(hear)	auditory, audience, audiophile
scrib	(write)	scribe, inscribe, describe
cede	(go)	recede, precede, secede
cise	(cut)	excise, incisive, incisors

Latin Stem Talk

AQUA means water. An *aquarium* is a tank of water with fish in it, *aquatic* means of the water, and an *aqueduct* was built by the Romans to bring water to the city!

AUDI means hear. Your *auditory* nerves help you hear, an *audience* will hear you, and an *audiophile* is a lover of stereo equipment!

SCRIB means write. A scribe is one who writes things down, to inscribe is to write something inside a book, and to describe is to write down a description.

CEDE means go. A flood goes back when it recedes, someone precedes you when they go first, and the South tried to secede from the Union in the Civil War by going apart!

CISE means cut. To excise is to cut out, to say something incisive is to say something that cuts into the issue, and incisors are teeth that cut!

Caesar's Analogy

The first two words are related to each other in a special way. Is one before the other? Is one inside the other? Are they opposites? Find the pair below that has the same relationship as the first pair!

SCRIBE : WRITES ::
  a. audience : hears
  b. audiophile : stereo
  c. incisive : speech
  d. aquarium : fish

Advanced Word: Aqueduct

The word **aqueduct** (awk-wa-dukt) contains the stems **aqua** (water) and **duct** (lead). The Romans built aqueducts, which were long channels that carried water from the mountain streams all the way down to Rome in the valley below. Some of the aqueducts were huge, and made of rows of arches on top of other rows of arches. At the very top of the aqueduct, above all of the arches, was the channel where the water flowed. Some of the Roman aqueducts are still standing today, two thousand years after they were built. One reason they were so strong is that the Romans invented concrete, which helped the rocks hold together over long periods of time.

Advanced Word: Incisive

One word that you are likely to read or hear is the adjective **incisive.** From the Latin *incisivus*, **incisive** usually refers to something that somebody says, and it means just what its stems suggest: cutting in. A comment or response that really cuts directly into the heart of the matter is incisive. One writer who loved this adjective was the great American novelist Henry James. In his novel *The American*, James wrote, "It was in this incisive strain that Mrs. Tristram moralised over Newman's so-called neglect." We also read, "You know how terribly incisive she is sometimes," and James described how a character, "dropped a series of softly-incisive comments upon her fellow-guests." One writer for younger readers who used the word **incisive** was James M. Barrie, the author of *Peter Pan*; Barrie wrote that "The order came sharp and incisive." Joseph Conrad used **incisive** several times in *Lord Jim*, and James Watson, a famous scientist who helped discover DNA, the chemical basis of life, wrote that "The chemists never provided anything incisive about the nucleic acids." Nucleic acids are important chemicals that are in the center, called the nucleus, of each cell in our bodies.

Which of these examples of **incisive** do you like the best?

How many different meanings of **incisive** do you see?

How many of these novels that use **incisive** have you heard of before?

The Catacombs

In the second century A.D., Christians in Rome began burying their dead under the ground. Little by little, these burial tombs increased in number and created a huge underground space. The catacombs are still there today.

Who's That Writer?

James D. Watson, whose middle name was *Dewey*, was born in 1928 in Chicago. He received a Ph.D. degree from Indiana University in 1950. In 1955 he began teaching at Harvard. In 1962 he and Francis Crick received the Nobel Prize for discovering the molecular structure of the DNA molecule, a structure of atoms that is the basis of life on Earth. In 1968 Watson wrote *The Double Helix*, telling the story of his work with Crick, and how they made their great discovery.

A Roman Fact

The emperor Octavian, called Augustus, was among the greatest of the Roman emperors. When he died, the Roman Empire covered 3,340 square miles, an area larger than the continental United States. This territory was over a hundred times larger than the Roman Empire before the Punic Wars with Carthage.

Caesar's Spanish

English and Spanish are very close modern relatives of ancient Latin. Look at the pairs of stems in these words:

stem	meaning	English / Spanish examples
aqua	(water)	aqueduct / acueducto
audi	(hear)	auditory / auditorio
scrib	(write)	inscribe / inscribir
cede	(go)	recede / retroceder
cise	(cut)	incisive / incisivo

Real Latin
From Cicero:

In virtute sunt multi ascensus.
There are many degrees in excellence.

Caesar's Word Search
In the box below, find the Latin-based English words. They might be vertical, horizontal, or at angles. Circle each word that you find.

```
V A U D I T O R Y N B I D V
A Q U A R I U M R D G C A G
L X F E N L E Q C I Y I E C
S N R V E D K I M G A N G F
C E I B E K T T F H U C R I
Z F C C B A C S P B D I Y N
L X E E U U E E X C I S E C
Z R S Q D D O P B I E O D I
P B A E E E W P A A N R M S
O E U C G T N G D W C S Y I
D Q E Y H S C R I B E H T V
A R J I N S C R I B E V E E
Q D E S C R I B E N L Z T B
A U D I O P H I L E T D P M
```

__ AQUATIC   __ AQUEDUCT   __ AQUARIUM   __ AUDITORY

__ AUDIENCE   __ AUDIOPHILE   __ SCRIBE   __ INSCRIBE

__ DESCRIBE   __ RECEDE   __ PRECEDE   __ SECEDE

__ EXCISE   __ INCISIVE   __ INCISORS

Review for Cumulative Quiz

bi	two	**sub**	under
de	down	**pre**	before
super	over	**un**	not
inter	between	**semi**	half
dis	away	**sym**	together
circum	around	**mal**	bad
post	after	**equi**	equal
ante	before	**aqua**	water
audi	hear	**scrib**	write
cede	go	**cise**	cut

countenance	facial expression	**profound**	deep
manifest	obvious	**prodigious**	huge
languor	weakness	**serene**	calm
acute	sharp	**grotesque**	distorted
condescend	to patronize	**odious**	hateful
exquisite	beautifully made	**clamor**	outcry
sublime	lofty	**tremulous**	quivering
allude	indirectly refer to		

A good man possesses a kingdom.

-Seneca
8 B.C. - 65 A.D.

Caesar's English
Vocabulary from Latin
Lesson Eight

1. **placid**: calm
2. **singular**: unique
3. **amiable**: friendly
4. **incredulous**: skeptical
5. **perplex**: confuse

placid

The peaceful English adjective **placid** means tranquil, calm, untroubled. We are pleased by the quiet and undisturbed feeling of a placid environment or a placid mind, and this is to be expected, since **placid** comes to us from the Romans' word *placidus*, a relative of *placere*, to please. **Placid** has variations such as the adverb **placidly** and the noun **placidity**, but it also has subtle word connections that may go unnoticed; when we **placate** someone, we make them placid, unless they are **implacable**.

Placid has been used by modern writers such as Sylvia Plath and Pearl Buck, by nineteenth century writers such as George Eliot, Harriet Beecher Stowe, and Charlotte Brontë, and by eighteenth century writers such as Mary Wollstonecraft.

Harper Lee wrote about a "placid week," Martin Luther King wrote about a "placid spring," and Marjorie Kinnan Rawlings wrote about a "deep and placid river." In Grahame's *The Wind in the Willows* there are "lakes so blue and placid," and a face that "wore a placid, satisfied expression." What do you think this means, when we describe a face as placid? In James M. Barrie's *Peter Pan* we read that "Even then Mrs. Darling was placid." In *Dracula*, Bram Stoker writes, "I found Renfield sitting placidly in his room with his hands folded, smiling benignly." Long John Silver, in Robert Louis Stevenson's *Treasure Island*, is seen "standing placidly by." And in Sir Walter Scott's *Ivanhoe* we learn that Cedric "was in no very placid state of mind." In Mary Shelley's novel *Frankenstein*, there is a sentence that contains our words **exquisite** and **placid**, and also the great word **verdure**, which means greenery. Shelley writes that a river, "the lovely Isis, which flows beside it through meadows of exquisite verdure, is spread forth into a placid expanse of waters." Exquisite verdure?

singular

The origin of the English word **singular**, though not simple, is *simple*. That is, the dictionary traces **singular** back to the Latin *singularis*, and tells us to look up *single*, which is traced back to the Latin *singulus*, at which point the dictionary tells us to look up *simple*, which traces back to the Latin *simplus/simplex*, at which point the dictionary tells us to look up *simplex*, which turns out to be Latin for one-fold, with *sim* meaning one and *plex* meaning fold! The meaning of **singular** is what you would expect: single in nature. Something that is singular can be unique, extraordinary, strange, or exceptional.

In Frances Hodgson Burnett's novel, *The Secret Garden*, "Colin had read about a great many singular things and was somehow a very convincing sort of boy." Burnett also writes that "A wind was rising and making a singular, wild, low, rushing sound." In *The Wind in the Willows*, we read that "Toad is busily arraying himself in those singularly hideous habiliments so dear to him." In Kingston's translation of Wyss's *The Swiss Family Robinson*, there is "the most singular-looking creature I ever beheld." Robert Louis Stevenson, in *Kidnapped*, writes that "Both Mr. Riach and the captain were singularly patient." In *Gulliver's Travels*, Jonathan Swift wrote that Gulliver had "never till then seen a race of mortals so singular in their shapes, habits, and countenances."

amiable

The adjective **amiable** comes from the Latin *amicabilis*, friendly, which came from the Latin *amicus*, friend, which was related to the Latin *amare*, to love. **Amiable** means friendly, good-natured, or agreeable. The word is one of the greatest English classic words; it has been in constant literary use since the 1300s, when Chaucer used it in *The Canterbury Tales*. It was also used by some of the other great early writers in English literature, such as William Shakespeare, Christopher Marlowe, and by John Milton, who wrote the great epic poem *Paradise Lost*. In modern times, it has been used by Toni Morrison, who won the Nobel prize for literature. Kenneth Grahame used it to describe "your amiable friend Mole," and Marjorie Kinnan Rawlings used it in *The Yearling* to describe Jody's mother: "Jody had never seen her so amiable." Rawlings also describes bear cubs: "The cubs made now and then an amiable talking." In *Peter Pan,* Peter calls Tink's name amiably. In Harper Lee's novel, *To Kill a Mockingbird*, we read that "He waited in amiable silence." And Jonathan Swift used **amiable** in his famous *Gulliver's Travels*, a great book for children that can be reread all of one's life; Swift wrote that "Truth appeared so amiable to me that I determined upon sacrificing everything to it."

A very interesting sentence comes from novelist Henry James, who uses **amiable** in his 1876 novel *The American*. James also uses our word **countenance** and the interesting word **saturnine**, which means distant and remote, like the planet Saturn. James writes that "His countenance, by daylight, had a sort of amiably saturnine cast." Does it seem strange to you that someone could be saturnine and amiable at the same time?

incredulous

The dubious adjective **incredulous**, meaning full of disbelief, reached the English language from the shores of Italy. In other words, like the other words we have studied, **incredulous** comes from ancient Latin, where it was the Roman word *incredulus*. In 2,000 years, we have added one *o* to the word.

Incredulous is part of a great family of words in English, including *credulous*, *credulity*, *incredulity*, *credible*, *incredible*, *credit*, *creditable*, *credo*, *discredit*, *creed*, and even *miscreant*. The key to all of these words is that the stem *cred* means belief.

It is interesting that **incredulous** comes to English later than most words we have studied. Even the *Oxford English Dictionary*, which often traces words from the 13th century, gives no examples of usage before the late 1500s. The first use of **incredulous** in the books we have mentioned is in Jane Austen's *Pride and Prejudice*, which wasn't written until 1813! In that book, there is an "audience not merely wondering but incredulous," a "smile of affected incredulity," and a moment where Elizabeth looks "at her sister with incredulous solicitude." **Solicitude** is concern.

In Grahame's *The Wind in the Willows*, something happens "full in view of the astonished and hitherto incredulous Mole." In the great American philosophical essay, *Walden*, Henry David Thoreau says that "My friends used to listen with incredulity when I told them." James Fennimore Cooper employs a huge vocabulary in his adventure novel, *The Last of the Mohicans*. In one of his sentences, Cooper writes that "Magua shook his head incredulously."

One of the most famous sentences in all of English literature occurs in Charles Dickens's *A Tale of Two Cities*, in which Dickens describes the French Revolution as "the epoch of incredulity." An epoch is an age, a period of years. Why do you think that Dickens would have called this period of great revolution an epoch of incredulity?

perplex

The verb **perplex** comes from the Latin *perplexus*, in which *per* meant thoroughly, and plexus meant *involved*. Does **perplex** still mean thoroughly involved today? Usually, no. To perplex is to bewilder, confuse, or puzzle. The idea is that the perplexed person is lost, completely unable to grasp something or to think clearly about it. In his 1667 masterpiece, *Paradise Lost*, John Milton writes of "perplexing thoughts." In 1719 Daniel Defoe writes, in *Robinson Crusoe*, "And yet here I was perplexed again." Emily Brontë combined two of our words in a sentence of *Wuthering Heights*, when her character speaks "with a perplexed countenance." Frederick Douglass writes, in his great *Narrative*, that "Our want of reverence for him must have perplexed him greatly." In *Tom Sawyer*, Mark Twain writes that "The school stared in perplexity at this incredible folly." Many other great children's novels use this word. Robert Louis Stevenson used it in *Treasure Island*, to describe "his face still wearing the expression of extreme perplexity." In Jack London's *The Call of the Wild*, we read that "The driver was perplexed." In Rouse's wonderful translation of *The Odyssey of Homer*, we read that "Saying this she went down the stairs with a heart full of perplexity."

Who's That Writer?

The English novelist Jane Austen wrote one of the most popular and influential novels of all time, *Pride and Prejudice*. Born in 1775 in Steventon, Hampshire, Austen wrote her first novel at the age of fourteen, and the bulk of her famous novels in her early twenties. Although she published numerous novels during her lifetime, no one knew it—she did not use her name, but only gave "By a Lady" as the author's identity. Jane Austen died in 1817, and is buried in Winchester Cathedral.

Real Latin

Pila ludere.
To play ball.

What Is This Writer Saying?

Discuss the meaning of the **bold** word in each of the following sentences:

From Joseph Conrad's *The Heart of Darkness*: "The swift and indifferent **placidity** of that look troubled me."

From Upton Sinclair's *The Jungle:* "Jurgis was no longer **perplexed** when he heard men talk of fighting for their rights."

From Rachel Carson's *Silent Spring*: "Our attitude toward plants is a **singularly** narrow one."

From Scott Fitzgerald's *The Great Gatsby*: "My **incredulity** was submerged into fascination now."

From Stephen Crane's *The Red Badge of Courage*: "In a short while the three antagonists could be seen together in an **amiable** bunch."

amiable

friendly, good-natured

The cubs made
now and then
an amiable talking.

-Marjorie Kinnan Rawlings
The Yearling

Caesar's Spanish

Everywhere we turn, language reveals to us that modern English and modern Spanish are both descendants of ancient Latin:

Latin	Spanish	English
placidus	plácido	placid
singularis	singular	singular
amicabilis	amable	amiable
incredulus	incrédulo	incredulous
perplexus	perplejo	perplex

Caesar's Synonyms

Here are words that are similar to the words in our list, but are they exactly the same in meaning? Or are they slightly different? For each word on our list, look up any synonym that you do not know, then pick one, and carefully explain the difference between it and our word.

placid: serene, calm, halcyon, peaceful, still, unruffled, even, quiet, unperturbed, impassive

singular: unique, particular, individual, differentiated, separate, discontinuous, discrete

amiable: genial, cordial, amicable, convivial, affable, sociable, friendly, personable, approachable

incredulous: doubting, questioning, skeptical, challenging, disbelieving, suspecting, uncertain, mistrustful

perplex: bewilder, baffle, confuse, mystify, befuddle, dumbfound, distract, stump, addle, stymie, muddle, elude

A Wordy Story...

With an acute alertness, the scientist peered through the tremulous leaves at the placid surface of the lake. Something prodigious and grotesque, she could sense, was stirring out there, and her countenance took on a profound perplexity as she shook off her afternoon languor and peered, incredulous, looking for something odious, something singular, something...but nothing was manifest. A blue jay clamored in the treetop. The wind made a sublime whisper of promise in the pines. What could be out there? She dared not even allude to it, even in her own mind. As she gazed at the lake, she realized that her thoughts were no longer serene; they were perturbed, and she waited impatiently for something to appear. And then, there it was: the ferry to the mainland, coming to take her off the island. With an amiable laugh, she ran down the trail to the beach.

Caesar's Rewrites

Here are some sentences from famous books. In each case, rewrite the sentence into more ordinary words. Example from Marjorie Rawlings's *The Yearling*: "A languor crept over him." The rewrite: Little by little, he began to feel lazy.

From Harper Lee's *To Kill A Mockingbird*: "He waited in **amiable** silence."

From Kenneth Grahame's *The Wind in the Willows*: "His face wore a **placid**, satisfied expression."

From Frances Hodgson Burnett's *The Secret Garden*: "A wind was rising and making a **singular**, wild, low, rushing sound."

From William Golding's *The Lord of the Flies*: "They were twins, and the eye was shocked and **incredulous** at such cheery duplication."

From Mark Twain's *Tom Sawyer*: "The school stared in **perplexity** at this incredible folly."

Caesar's Favorite Word

Think carefully about each of the words in this lesson, and predict which of Caesar's words you think you will use most often. Explain why you made this word your choice, and give at least three examples of situations in which you could use that word.

Caesar's Antonyms

For each of the words in this lesson, think of a word that means the opposite. A word that means the opposite is known as an antonym.

1. **placid**
2. **singular**
3. **amiable**
4. **incredulous**
5. **perplex**

Are there any words in this list that have no antonyms? Are there any that it is very difficult to think of an antonym for? Why?

Caesar's Analogies

Analogies are about relationships. Find a second pair of words that have the same relationship to each other as the first pair has. Remember that it sometimes helps to put the two words into a sentence that makes the relationship clear.

MIRACLE : INCREDULOUS ::

a. placid : serene
b. singular : common
c. mystery : perplexed
d. allude : refer

Coins, with Mars depicted.

Review for Cumulative Quiz

bi	two	**sub**	under
de	down	**pre**	before
super	over	**un**	not
inter	between	**semi**	half
dis	away	**sym**	together
circum	around	**mal**	bad
post	after	**equi**	equal
ante	before	**aqua**	water
audi	hear	**scrib**	write
cede	go	**cise**	cut

countenance	facial expression	**profound**	deep
manifest	obvious	**prodigious**	huge
languor	weakness	**serene**	calm
acute	sharp	**grotesque**	distorted
condescend	to patronize	**odious**	hateful
exquisite	beautifully made		
clamor	outcry		
sublime	lofty		
tremulous	quivering		
allude	indirectly refer to		
placid	calm		
singular	unique		
amiable	friendly		
incredulous	skeptical		
perplex	confuse		

Caesar's English
Ancient Latin Stems
Lesson Nine

Latin Stem List

stem	meaning	modern examples
cred	(believe)	incredulous, credo, credible
miss	(send)	missive, remiss, emission
cide	(kill)	regicide, homicide, fratricide
dict	(say)	edict, malediction, contradict
bell	(war)	rebellion, bellicose, belligerent

Latin Stem Talk

CRED means believe. When we can't believe someone, we are *incredulous*, a *credo* (pronounced kreedo) is a set of beliefs, and something is *credible* when it is believable!

MISS means send. A *missive* is a letter that you send, to be *remiss* in your duty means that we have to send you back to do it again, and an *emission* is like car exhaust, that is sent out!

CIDE means kill. To kill a king is *regicide*, to kill a human is *homicide*, and to kill a brother is *fratricide*!

DICT means say. An *edict* is an official public statement that has the force of law, a *malediction* is a curse, and to *contradict* is to say something against another's statement.

BELL means war. A *rebellion* is a war of opposition, the adjective *bellicose* means extremely warlike, and *belligerent* is another word that means warlike and hostile!

Caesar's Analogy

The first two words are related to each other in a special way. Is one before the other? Is one inside the other? Are they opposites? Find the pair below that has the same relationship as the first pair!

REGICIDE : HOMICIDE ::
  a. missive : communication
  b. incredulous : gullible
  c. friendly : furious
  d. malediction : blessing

Advanced Word: Bellicose

The adjective **bellicose** (bell-ih-kose), from the Latin *bellicosus*, contains the stems **bell** (war) and **ose** (full of). **Bellicose** means really warlike, inclined to start quarrels or wars. In her great book about nature and the danger of chemical pesticides, *Silent Spring*, Rachel Carson wrote that honeybees that have contacted pesticides become "wildly agitated and bellicose." A good synonym for **bellicose** is the adjective **pugnacious,** which means wanting to fight.

Advanced Word: Missive

From the Latin missive, our English noun **missive** refers to a letter, which is, as the stem **miss** suggests, sent. We can see how the stem **miss** provides a synthetic connection to other words: a missive is *sent*, to dismiss is to *send* a way, a missile is *sent* toward the enemy, if you are remiss in your duty we *send* you back, emissions are *sent* out of an engine, a missionary is *sent* abroad, and so forth. The idea of being sent, like a missive, is what connects all of these words. In Shakespeare's 1606 masterpiece, *Macbeth,* there were "missives from the king, who all-hail'd me 'Thane of Cawdor.'" In 1847, Thackeray used **missive** in *Vanity Fair* several times, writing once that "She took up the black-edged missive," that the character "perused the missive," and also that "this authentic missive was despatched under cover to Miss Briggs." In her 1847 classic (notice that this is the same year *Vanity Fair* was published) *Wuthering Heights*, Emily Brontë described how a character was fearful "lest it should be imagined a missive of my own" and how a character tries "to prevail on myself to put the missive into Mrs. Linton's hand." In Melville's 1851 *Moby Dick*, a character takes "the fatal missive from Starbuck's hands."

Who's That Writer?

Toni Morrison was born in Lorain, Ohio, in 1931. Her work expresses the black experience in America, and is filled with detailed observation and deep compassion. She earned an M.A. degree in English at Cornell University in 1955 and taught at Texas Southern University and Howard University before becoming an editor at Random House, one of the great publishing firms. Her novels, such as *Song of Solomon* and *Beloved* earned her the Nobel Prize for literature in 1993.

Caesar's Spanish

stem	meaning	English / Spanish examples
cred	(believe)	incredulous / incrédulo
miss	(send)	missive / misivo
cide	(kill)	regicide / regicidio
dict	(say)	edict / edicto
bell	(war)	bellicose / belicoso

Roman Fact

Lucius Annaeus Seneca, a Stoic philosopher, was born in what is now Spain in 4 B.C. He wrote that we should read philosophers, not just the outlines of philosophy—the full original works. He also told us that we should read good books many times, rather than many books. Why do you think he gave us this advice?

Real Latin

Quo plura habemus, eo cupimus ampliora.

The more we have,
the more we want.

Caesar's Word Search

In the box below, find the Latin-based English words. They might be vertical, horizontal, or at angles. Circle each word that you find.

```
V N E X H O M I C I D E E T
E B V D B N H N P I R K F M
M E V X I H L L W N E B M A
I L K C H C F A E C G E C L
S L G A C C T L G R I L O E
S I C P R G B K N E C L N D
I C K C E I G O S D I I T I
O O J D D E I S E U D G R C
N S H E O L I V O L E E A T
U E R I L M I Z G O M R D I
S C X E E S V P R U T E I O
S N B R S M L O R S B N C N
H E Y I C S V M R C W T T M
R G M F R A T R I C I D E S
```

___ INCREDULOUS ___ CREDO ___ CREDIBLE ___ MISSIVE
___ REMISS ___ EMISSION ___ REGICIDE ___ HOMICIDE
___ FRATRICIDE ___ EDICT ___ MALEDICTION ___ CONTRADICT
___ REBELLION ___ BELLICOSE ___ BELLIGERENT

Julius Caesar, from his *Commentaries on the Gallic Wars*:

There is nothing surprising in the Gauls' readiness to revolt. Tribes that were thought the bravest in the world felt bitter resentment at the loss of this reputation that submission to Rome created.

Review for Cumulative Quiz

bi	two	**sub**	under
de	down	**pre**	before
super	over	**un**	not
inter	between	**semi**	half
dis	away	**sym**	together
circum	around	**mal**	bad
post	after	**equi**	equal
ante	before	**aqua**	water
audi	hear	**scrib**	write
cede	go	**cise**	cut
cred	believe	**miss**	send
cide	kill	**dict**	say
bell	war		

countenance	facial expression	**profound**	deep
manifest	obvious	**prodigious**	huge
languor	weakness	**serene**	calm
acute	sharp	**grotesque**	distorted
condescend	to patronize	**odious**	hateful
exquisite	beautifully made	**clamor**	outcry
sublime	lofty	**tremulous**	quivering
allude	indirectly refer to	**placid**	calm
singular	unique	**amiable**	friendly
incredulous	skeptical	**perplex**	confuse

Think of
your ancestors
and
your posterity.

- Tacitus
54-119 A.D.

Caesar's English
Vocabulary from Latin
Lesson Ten

1. **melancholy**: sadness
2. **visage**: the face
3. **venerate**: to respect
4. **abate**: to lessen
5. **repose**: resting

melancholy

The English noun **melancholy** comes from the Latin *melancholia*, which came from the ancient Greek *mela*, black, and *chole*, bile. The idea was that sadness or dejection is caused by an excess of black bile in the body—something that we now know is not true. The idea, however, has survived in the word. **Melancholy** is a very old word in English literature. Chaucer used it as far back as 1385, saying that the "humour of malencolye causeth ful many a man in sleep to crye." William Shakespeare used it in many of his plays. In *As You Like It*, written in 1599, he wrote that "The melancholy Jacques grieves at that." In his 1601 masterpiece, *Hamlet*, the villainous uncle Claudius notes of Prince Hamlet that "There's something in his soul, o'er which his melancholy sits on brood." In Jonathan Swift's 1726 *Gulliver's Travels*, Gulliver writes that "I rose up with as melancholy a disposition as ever I had in my life." In Lewis Carroll's 1865 story *Alice in Wonderland*, we read that "she had put the Lizard in head downwards, and the poor little thing was waving its tail about in a melancholy way." In Robert Louis Stevenson's *Treasure Island*, written in 1881, we read about "the look of the island, with its grey, melancholy woods." In Jack London's 1903 *The Call of the Wild*, there is "the melancholy rippling of waves on lonely beaches." We can see from these famous uses of the word that melancholy can describe a person's feelings, but it can also describe things in the environment that seem sad, or that make us feel sad. One of the most striking **melancholy** sentences comes from 1904, from James M. Barrie's great *Peter Pan*: "His eyes were of the blue of the forget-me-not, and of a profound melancholy."

visage

The English noun **visage** is a synonym of our friend **countenance**. Perhaps there is a difference in emphasis in the words, with **countenance** focusing on the contents of the expression and **visage** emphasizing the look of the face; after all, **visage** traces back to the Latin *videre*, to see. Even so, the two words both refer to the appearance of the face, and **countenance** is often used to define **visage**. We see from literature that the visage can be pale, comely, plump, or doleful. It can be domineering or stern. Chaucer described a "sad visage," and Shakespeare wrote a wonderful description of a mask in *Romeo and Juliet*: "Give me a case" he wrote, "to put my visage in." In *Paradise Lost*, the greatest epic poem in the English language, John Milton wrote of "Celestial visages," a "visage all inflamed," and a "visage incompos'd." In Sir Walter Scott's knight novel, *Ivanhoe*, we read of the "scars with which his visage was seamed." And in Mary Shelley's *Frankenstein*, the poor monster explains that "I travelled only at night, fearful of encountering the visage of a human being." In James Fennimore Cooper's *The Last of the Mohicans*, we encounter "the scowling visage of Chingachgook." One of the greatest **visage** sentences comes from the great English novelist Charles Dickens, who in *A Tale of Two Cities* described someone's "taciturn and iron-bound visage." *Taciturn* means silent, and so this character's visage is frozen and metallic—not very pleasant!

venerate

To **venerate** is to respect or revere, to admire. The word traces all the way back to the Roman's word *venus*, love. **Veneration** is a kind of high, respectful love. The adjective form of the word is **venerable**. It is important for many words to see that they are available in different part of speech: **venerate** is a verb, **veneration** is a noun, **venerable** is an adjective. Being able to change forms like this gives a word great power in our sentences. What kinds of things can we venerate? What things can be venerable? In British and American literature, there are venerable white beards, venerable towns, venerable bows of ships, and venerable friends. We often use **venerable** to describe what is religious; there are venerable ministers, venerable pastors, and venerable chapels. In *Walden*, Henry David Thoreau wrote of a "venerable moss-grown and hoary ruin." In *Song of Myself*, part of his great *Leaves of Grass*, Walt Whitman asked, "Why should I venerate and be ceremonious?" Sometimes veneration is very sincere; In *Uncle Tom's Cabin*, Harriet Beecher Stowe described a character who was "gazing upward with a face fervent with veneration." The word *fervent* means that the face was very intense, very sincere. In Sir Walter Scott's *Ivanhoe*, we also see this kind of earnest veneration; another character had extended "his hand to Gurth, who kissed it with the utmost possible veneration." In *Gulliver's Travels*, Jonathan Swift had his main character Gulliver admit that "I have too great a veneration for crowned heads." In Charlotte Brontë's great novel *Jane Eyre*, Jane confesses that "I deeply venerated my cousin's talent and principle."

abate

Our English verb **abate** means to lessen in amount or degree, but it comes from the Old French *abattre*, to beat down! This, in turn, came from the Latin *batuere*, to beat. Writers have used **abate** to describe how things go down, reduce, or recede. Note that in order for something to get smaller, it must first be bigger, and so **abate** is what big things do. Big storms abate. Big emotions abate. In Bram Stoker's *Dracula* we read, "When the snow storm abated we looked again." In Kingston's translation of Wyss's *The Swiss Family Robinson*, we read that "Toward evening the universal excitement began to abate, and the party assembled for supper with tolerable composure." In Robert Louis Stevenson's *Kidnapped*, we read that "my strength had much abated." In Scott's *Ivanhoe*, we are relieved to learn that "His fever is abated." Mary Shelley, in *Frankenstein*, wrote that "I continued with unabated fervour to traverse immense deserts." This is a great sentence for us to study because it contains not only the negative of **abate**, but it also contains **traverse,** another word in this lesson. **Traverse** means cross, and so *traversing a desert* is crossing it. In Shakespeare's great tragedy, *King Lear*, the pitiful old king complains that his daughter has gotten rid of his train, his group of servants: "She hath abated me of half my train," he cries.

repose

The English word **repose** traces all the way back to the Latin *pausa*, to pause. When we re-pose, we pause again. When we use **repose** as a verb, it means the act of resting, and when we use **repose** as a noun, it refers to the rest. In Shakespeare's 1611 play *The Tempest*, a character sleepwalks: "This is a strange repose, to be asleep with eyes wide open—standing, speaking, moving, and yet so fast asleep." Two hundred years after Shakespeare, Mary Shelley used **repose** in *Frankenstein*, to paint a picture of tranquility: "All nature reposed under the eye of the quiet moon." In *The Legend of Sleepy Hollow*, Washington Irving wrote that "A small brook glides through it, with just murmur enough to lull one to repose." An interesting use comes from Sir Walter Scott in *Ivanhoe*, where the knights take the trouble "to repose their horses." Robert Louis Stevenson used **repose** in *Dr. Jekyll and Mr. Hyde*, to describe the repose of an inanimate (mindless) object: "He locked the note into his safe, where it reposed from that time forward." In Frances Hodgson Burnett's *The Secret Garden* there is "a new reposeful sleep." In Kenneth Grahame's *The Wind in the Willows* there is a "well-earned repose." And in George Orwell's *Animal Farm* "Napoleon reposed on a bed of straw." Napoleon, being a pig, needed his repose.

What Is This Writer Saying?

Discuss the meaning of the **bold** word in each of the following sentences:

From Joseph Conrad's *Heart of Darkness*: "A heap of rubbish **reposed** in a dark corner."

From William Shakespeare's *A Midsummer Night's Dream*: "O long and tedious night, **abate** thy hours!"

From Harper Lee's *To Kill a Mockingbird*: "The Maycomb jail was the most **venerable** of the county's buildings."

From Robert Penn Warren's *All the King's Men:* "Mr. Patton's granite **visage** seemed to lean toward me like a monument about to fall."

From William Shakespeare's *Hamlet:* "There's something in his soul, o'er which his **melancholy** sits on brood."

abate

lessen

O long and
tedious night,
abate thy hours.

-William Shakespeare
A Midsummer Night's Dream

Caesar's Synonyms

Here are words that are similar to the words in our list, but are they exactly the same in meaning? Or are they slightly different? For each word on our list, look up any synonym that you do not know, then pick one, and carefully explain the difference between it and our word.

melancholy: glumness, sadness, dejection, gloominess, woe, desolation, unhappiness, depression, despair

visage: expression, countenance, mien, air, physiognomy, aspect, look, mug, lineament, features

venerate: respect, honor, cherish, esteem, treasure, admire, prize, look up to, value, reverence, appreciate, revere, regard

abate: fade, flag, subside, mellow, ease, slacken, ebb, dwindle, recede, relent, taper, moderate, die down, wane, relent, fall, lapse

repose: rest, peace, respite, quiet, placidity, calmness, relaxation, lull, serenity, ease, stillness, breathing-space

Real Latin

From Horace:

Puella eximia forma.

A girl of exceptional beauty.

Caesar's Spanish

Everywhere we turn, language reveals to us that modern English and modern Spanish are both descendants of ancient Latin:

Latin	Spanish	English
melancholia	melancolía	melancholy
venus	venerar	venerate
reponere	reposo	repose

Caesar's Rewrites

Here are some sentences from famous books. In each case, rewrite the sentence into more ordinary words. Example from Marjorie Rawlings's *The Yearling*: "A languor crept over him." The rewrite: Little by little, he began to feel lazy.

From Jack London's *The Call of the Wild*: "His mane, in **repose** as it was, half bristled."

From Harper Lee's *To Kill A Mockingbird*: "The Maycomb jail was the most **venerable** of the county's buildings."

From Rouse's translation of *The Odyssey of Homer*: "How can we persuade Poseidon to **abate** his anger?"

From James M. Barrie's *Peter Pan*: "This ill-luck had given a gentle **melancholy** to his countenance."

From Frederick Douglass's *Narrative*: "The right of the grim-**visaged** pirate upon the high seas is exactly the same."

Who's That Writer?

Jonathan Swift wrote *Gulliver's Travels*, one of the world's most popular books for children and adults alike. Born in 1667 in Dublin, Ireland, Swift attended college at Trinity College, Dublin. In his early writing, he ridiculed shallow thinkers and supported the merits of the ancient classics. *Gulliver's Travels*, published anonymously in 1726, mocked the foibles of all mankind and was Swift's masterpiece. He died in 1745 and is buried in St. Patrick's Cathedral, Dublin.

melancholy

sadness

There's something
in his soul,
o'er which
his melancholy
sits on brood.

-William Shakespeare
Hamlet

Caesar's Antonyms

For each of the Caesar's English words in this lesson, think of a word that means the opposite. A word that means the opposite is known as an **antonym**.

1. **melancholy**
2. **visage**
3. **venerate**
4. **abate**
5. **repose**

Are there any words in this list that have no antonyms? Are there any that it is very difficult to think of an antonym for? Why?

Caesar's Analogies

Analogies are about relationships. Find a second pair of words that has the same relationship to each other as the first pair has. Remember that it sometimes helps to put the two words into a sentence that makes the relationship clear.

MELANCHOLY : VISAGE ::

a. repose : rest
b. traverse : space
c. abate : increase
d. vivid : color

STORM : ABATE ::

a. fear : diminish
b. traverse : cross
c. visage : handsome
d. melancholy : dejected

Review for Cumulative Quiz

bi	two	**sub**	under
de	down	**pre**	before
super	over	**un**	not
inter	between	**semi**	half
dis	away	**sym**	together
circum	around	**mal**	bad
post	after	**equi**	equal
ante	before	**aqua**	water
audi	hear	**scrib**	write
cede	go	**cise**	cut
cred	believe	**miss**	send
cide	kill	**dict**	say
bell	war		

countenance	facial expression	**profound**	deep
manifest	obvious	**prodigious**	huge
languor	weakness	**serene**	calm
acute	sharp	**grotesque**	distorted
condescend	to patronize	**odious**	hateful
exquisite	beautifully made	**clamor**	outcry
sublime	lofty	**tremulous**	quivering
allude	indirectly refer to	**placid**	calm
singular	unique	**amiable**	friendly
incredulous	skeptical	**perplex**	confuse
melancholy	sadness	**visage**	the face
venerate	to respect	**abate**	to lessen
repose	resting		

visage
the face or expression

Mr. Tristram puckered
his plump visage.

\- Henry James
The American

98   98

Caesar's English
Ancient Latin Stems
Lesson Eleven

Latin Stem List

stem	meaning	modern examples
spec	(look)	specter, specious, spectrum
pend	(hang)	pending, impending, depend
omni	(all)	omnipotent, omnivorous, omniscient
re	(again)	reiterate, regurgitate, revive
ex	(out)	exculpate, exorbitant, except

Latin Stem Talk

SPEC means look. A *specter* is something that appears, like a ghost, *specious* (pronounced speeshus) means true-looking but false anyway, and a *spectrum* is an array of colors!

PEND means hang. *Pending* means hanging in wait, like something not yet decided; *impending* means hanging over you, like a storm; and *depend* means to hang on or rely on something else for support!

OMNI means all. *Omnipotent* means all-powerful, like a god; *omnivorous* means eating everything, like human beings; and *omniscient* means all-knowing.

RE means again. To *reiterate* is to repeat again, to *regurgitate* is to spit back up again, and to *revive* is to bring back to life again!

EX means out. To *exculpate* someone is to free them from blame, *exorbitant* means outrageously high, and to *except* is to treat someone or something differently, in a special way!

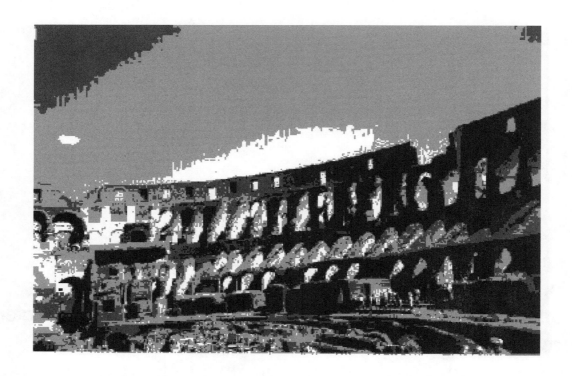

Caesar's Analogy

The first two words are related to each other in a special way. Is one before the other? Is one inside the other? Are they opposites? Find the pair below that has the same relationship as the first pair!

OMNIPOTENT : POWER ::
  a. omnivorous : teeth
  b. omniscient : everything
  c. omnivorous : hungry
  d. omniscient : knowledge

Advanced Words: Specious

The adjective **specious** means false, but not the kind of false that anyone can see; **specious** refers to something false that appears to be true! It is full of (ous) looks (spec), but it only looks good. We usually use **specious** to refer to thinking; we talk about specious reasoning and specious arguments. In 1792 Mary Wollstonecraft, the mother of the woman who wrote *Frankenstein*, described "specious prejudices."

Advanced Word: Omnipotent

Omnipotent, all-powerful, is a very old English word. From the Latin *omnipotens*, it was already in use when Chaucer wrote his epic poem, *The Canterbury Tales*, in 1385, over six hundred years ago; Chaucer described the "verray God, that is omnipotent." Notice that we don't spell *very* that way anymore. In 1667 poet John Milton described an "Omnipotent Decree," and in 1719 Daniel Defoe, in *Robinson Crusoe*, described "God, who was not only righteous but omnipotent." In *Ivanhoe* Sir Walter Scott described "that spell which his Jester had recommended as omnipotent." In modern American literature, Herman Melville used **omnipotent** in his great novel *Moby Dick* to describe the "vast swells of the omnipotent sea," and even to describe art! It would be good if everyone had so much faith in the power of art. In what way do you think art is omnipotent? In 1989 novelist John Gardner used **omnipotence**, the noun form of the word, in his novel *Grendel*; Gardner described the "omnipotence of words." In what way are words omnipotent?

Which of these examples of **omnipotent** do you like the best?

How many different meanings of **omnipotent** do you see?

How many of these novels that use **omnipotent** have you heard of before?

Who's That Writer?

Daniel Defoe was the author of the great adventure novel of shipwreck and survival, *Robinson Crusoe*, which was published in 1719, when Defoe was almost sixty years old. Born, probably, in 1660 in London, Defoe was the son of Mr. Foe, a candle merchant. Daniel added the *De* to his name in 1700. In 1701, Defoe wrote a poem, "The True-born Englishman" that attacked ideas of racial and national superiority. In 1703 he was jailed for his writings. *Robinson Crusoe* is based on the true story of Alexander Selkirk, who had been marooned off the coast of Chile, on one of the Juan Fernández Islands. It is now a classic of children's literature. Defoe died in 1731.

Caesar's Spanish

stem	meaning	English / Spanish examples
spec	(look)	specious / especioso
pend	(hang)	pending / pendiente
omni	(all)	omnipotent / omnipotente
re	(again)	reiterate / reiterar
ex	(out)	exculpate / exculpar

Roman Fact

When the Carthaginian general Hannibal led his elephants and army over the Alps and down into Italy, he was welcomed by the barbarian Gauls as a savior. It was a good thing for him; the trip through the mountains had cost him half his army, and he was reduced to only 26,000 troops. Against this force, Rome sent over 300,000 men. Eventually, Hannibal was driven from Italy.

Real Latin

Omnes virtutes jacent, volupate dominate.
All virtues lie prostrate if pleasure is the master.

Caesar's Word Search

In the box below, find the Latin-based English words. They might be vertical, horizontal, or at angles. Circle each word that you find.

```
S I M P E N D I N G D G F U
E W I R P E N D I N G D E L
R L A O E S U Z I K N A X E
O E D W M I P Q F E Y O C X
E M G J U N T E P R D J U O
Y S N U S J I E C W B C L R
T Y P I R P D S R T L V P B
E I R E P G E O C A E Y A I
X Q E Y C O I C X I T R T T
C I V O W T T T I G E E E A
E S I F S C R E A O U N I N
P I V L T P H U N T U U T T
T P E T L Y V O M T E S F D
O M N I V O R O U S I E P W
```

___ SPECTER   ___ SPECIOUS   ___ SPECTRUM   ___ PENDING

___ IMPENDING   ___ DEPEND   ___ OMNIPOTENT   ___ OMNIVOROUS

___ OMNISCIENT   ___ REITERATE   ___ REGURGITATE   ___ REVIVE

___ EXCULPATE   ___ EXORBITANT   ___ EXCEPT

Julius Caesar, from his *Commentaries on the Gallic Wars*:

The Roman soldiers were unnerved by the shouts they could hear behind them in the fight, that proved their lives depended on the bravery of others.

Review for Cumulative Quiz

bi	two	**sub**	under
de	down	**pre**	before
super	over	**un**	not
inter	between	**semi**	half
dis	away	**sym**	together
circum	around	**mal**	bad
post	after	**equi**	equal
ante	before	**aqua**	water
audi	hear	**scrib**	write
cede	go	**cise**	cut
cred	believe	**miss**	send
cide	kill	**dict**	say
bell	war	**spec**	look
pend	hang	**omni**	all
re	again	**ex**	out

countenance	facial expression	**profound**	deep
manifest	obvious	**prodigious**	huge
languor	weakness	**serene**	calm
acute	sharp	**grotesque**	distorted
condescend	to patronize	**odious**	hateful
exquisite	beautifully made	**clamor**	outcry
sublime	lofty	**tremulous**	quivering
allude	indirectly refer to	**placid**	calm
singular	unique	**amiable**	friendly
incredulous	skeptical	**perplex**	confuse
melancholy	sadness	**visage**	the face
venerate	to respect	**abate**	to lessen
repose	resting		

It is well to moor your bark with two anchors.

- Publius Syrius
42 B.C.

Caesar's English
Vocabulary from Latin
Lesson Twelve

1. **vulgar**: common
2. **traverse**: to cross
3. **undulate**: to wave
4. **vivid**: bright
5. **pallor**: paleness

vulgar

Our adjective **vulgar** is what survives of the ancient Latin word *vulgus*, mob. When we say something is **vulgar**, we are saying it is common, lacking in good taste or refinement. In the great works of British and American literature, there are vulgar money-getters, vulgar hotels, vulgar superstitions, vulgar hats, and vulgar emotions. In Kenneth Grahame's *The Wind in the Willows* there are vulgar songs. Oscar Wilde wrote about vulgar realism, and described how the "vulgar directness of the question called for a direct answer." In Mark Twain's *Tom Sawyer* someone "called Tom a bad, vicious, vulgar child." In writing about the ancient world in his American classic *Walden*, Henry David Thoreau wrote that "The grandeur of Thebes was a vulgar grandeur." Walter Scott wrote of "the poor as well as the rich, the vulgar as well as the noble." Although we usually use **vulgar** as an adjective, sometimes it is used as a noun; in *Frankenstein* Mary Shelley wrote that "Astounding horror would be looked upon as madness by the vulgar," referring to the mob of villagers. One of America's greatest writers is Nathaniel Hawthorne, the author of *The Scarlet Letter*. In one of his other novels, *The House of the Seven Gables*, Hawthorne used **vulgar** very creatively, to describe how someone was "driven away by no less vulgar a dissonance than the ringing of the shop bell." A dissonance is a bad sound, one that is not harmonious to the ear. A great sentence comes from Jonathan Swift's *Gulliver's Travels*, where some things are known to be important, "however insignificant they may appear to groveling vulgar minds." Perhaps the most famous **vulgar** sentence of all comes from perhaps the most famous literary masterwork of all, Shakespeare's great play *Hamlet*. In *Hamlet*, the tedious old fool Polonius instructs his son Laertes how to act: "Be thou familiar, but by no means vulgar." The foolish advice is impossible to follow.

traverse

The English verb **traverse** comes from the Latin *transversus*, meaning to turn across. In English, **traverse** is to cross, as we noticed in our discussion of **abate**. We can find **traverse** used in a myriad (wide variety) of creative ways. E.L. Doctorow described "a bluebottle fly traversing the screen" and on the ocean "a small craft slowly traversing the horizon." Maya Angelou wrote how one "learned to traverse the maze of Spanish-named streets in that enigma that is Los Angeles." Sylvia Plath wrote a beautiful, haunting sentence about how "Every so often a beam of light appeared out of thin air, traversed the wall like a ghostly, exploratory finger, and slid off into nothing again." Mark Twain used **traverse** in *Tom Sawyer* to explain how "his mind was traversing the whole field of human thought." He also described how "Nudges and winks and whispers traversed the room." Sir Walter Scott used **traverse** in *Ivanhoe* to describe a vivid sound: "The heavy yet hasty step of the men-at-arms traversed the battlements." The great English novelist Thomas Hardy used **traverse** in *The Return of the Native* to describe a panoramic view of the English landscape: "The above-mentioned highway traversed the lower levels of the heath, from one horizon to the another." He also described how one of his characters was "soon ascending Blooms-End valley and traversing the undulations on the side of the hill." An undulation, as we shall see in our next word, is a wave, and so the undulations on the side of the hill are the wavy shapes of the hillside.

undulate

To the Romans, an *undula* was a small wave. Two thousand years later, we still say that something that waves **undulates**. **Undulate**, or its noun form, **undulation**, can describe anything that moves in a wave-form, but it can also describe something that intensifies and then abates repeatedly, such as light: John Gardner once wrote about the "undulant, dragon-red light." **Undulate** can also describe sound, such as when Jean Craighead George used it in *Julie of the Wolves*: "Jello whined an undulating note and Kapu turned back to the den." Authors often use **undulate** to describe a hilly landscape; in *A Separate Peace* John Knowles described how "The last long rays of light played across the campus, accenting every slight undulation of the land." James M. Barrie also used the word this way in *Peter Pan*, describing "a rude stockade on the summit of yonder undulating ground." Our voices can **undulate**; in Thomas Hardy's *The Mayor of Casterbridge*, a sentence is "uttered in his undulatory accents," and we learn that "Donald's voice musically undulated between two semitones." In Hardy's *The Return of the Native* he beautifully described "two or three undulating locks of raven hair." Thoreau referred to the "undulations of celestial music." In *Frankenstein*, Mary Shelley even used **undulation** to describe a glacier: "I saw him [the monster] descend the mountain with greater speed than the flight of an eagle, and quickly lost him among the undulations of the sea of ice."

vivid

Our adjective **vivid** is a distant echo of the Latin *vivere*, to live. Something that is **vivid** is bright, colorful, lifelike. **Vivid** things make strong impressions on us. When our imaginations are **vivid**, they give us images that are convincing and believable, like real life. In British and American literature, we can find long, vivid gowns; a vivid, dark-eyed girl, and drops of vivid blood. William Golding wrote about "the vivid phantoms of his day-dream," and Scott Fitzgerald wrote about "bedrooms swathed in rose and lavender silk and vivid with new flowers." In his modern novel *1984*, George Orwell wrote that "Vivid, beautiful hallucinations flashed through his mind." The idea in that sentence is that even though they were only hallucinations, they were so lifelike that they seemed real. Sometimes **vivid** just means very colorful or intense; in H.G. Wells's *The War of the Worlds*, about a Martian invasion of the Earth, there is "a vivid red glare." Wells used the word repeatedly, describing "a vivid sense of danger," "puffs of vivid green vapor," "a vivid account of the Heat-Ray," and "a vivid blood-red tint." Herman Melville, in *Moby Dick*, described "That unblinkingly vivid Japanese sun." One of the most interesting **vivid** sentences comes from Mary Shelley, who wrote in *Frankenstein* that "My imagination was vivid, yet my powers of analysis and application were intense."

pallor

The English noun **pallor** comes from the Latin *pallere*, to be pale. **Pallor** is a noun; its adjective form is **pallid**. The most frequent use of **pallor** is to describe the gray face of someone who is sick, weak, or afraid. Sylvia Plath wrote of "a pallid man in a shabby maroon bathrobe." Joseph Conrad wrote of "the even olive pallor of her complexion." Bram Stoker wrote that "the cheeks had the warmth of life through all their pallor." Stephen Crane wrote that "His face was of a clammy pallor." In *The Return of the Native*, Thomas Hardy wrote that "The pallid Eustacia said nothing." In *Tom Sawyer*, Mark Twain wrote that "The moon drifted from behind the clouds and exposed the pallid face." In *Jane Eyre*, Charlotte Brontë wrote that "Mr. Rochester's extreme pallor had disappeared." Robert Louis Stevenson, in *Dr. Jekyll and Mr. Hyde*, described the butler, "turning to a sort of mottled pallor." One of the great sentences comes from Walt Whitman's *Leaves of Grass*; Whitman describes: "The judge with hands tight to the desk, his pallid lips pronouncing a death-sentence."

Although **pallor** often describes the face, it can be used in other ways. In *Moby Dick* Melville wrote that "All the yard-arms [of the ship] were tipped with a pallid fire." H.G. Wells wrote of "the dying moonlight and the first pallor of dawn." Robert Louis Stevenson gave us a chilling image of Mr. Hyde's **pallid** hand: "the hand…was…of a dusky pallor and thickly shaded with a swart growth of hair."

Who's That Author?

Maya Angelou, the author of *I Know Why the Caged Bird Sings*, was born in 1928 in St. Louis, Missouri. Her real name is Marguerite Annie Johnson, but she was named *My-a-sister* by her older brother. Her first job was as a streetcar conductor in San Francisco. Turning to dance, she moved to New York and toured the world in a production of George Gershwin's *Porgy and Bess*, and even studied with Martha Graham. Her first book, *I Know Why the Caged Bird Sings*, gave her fame as a writer, and was nominated for the National Book Award. Maya Angelou has received international acclaim, has over fifty honorary degrees, and read her own poem, "On the Pulse of Morning," at the inauguration of President William Jefferson Clinton—the first American poet to be so honored since Robert Frost read at the inauguration of John Fitzgerald Kennedy.

Caesar's Spanish

Everywhere we turn, language reveals to us that modern English and modern Spanish are both descendants of ancient Latin:

Latin	Spanish	English
vividus	vívido	vivid
undulatus	ondulado	undulate
transversare	atravesar	traverse
pallidus	pálido	pallid
vulgaris	vulgar	vulgar

What Is This Writer Saying?

Discuss the meaning of the **bold** word in each of the following sentences:

From William Golding's *Lord of the Flies*: "He was a skinny, **vivid** little boy."

From John Knowles's *A Separate Peace*: "The playing fields swept away from me in slight frosty **undulations** which bespoke meanings upon meanings."

From James Joyce's *A Portrait of the Artist as a Young Man*: "The image of Mercedes **traversed** the background of his memory."

From William Golding's *The Lord of the Flies*: "The choir boy who had fainted sat up against a palm trunk, smiled **pallidly** at Ralph, and said that his name was Simon."

From Thomas Hardy's *The Return of the Native*: "Isolation on a heath renders **vulgarity** well-nigh impossible."

undulate

to wave

The ice undulated under a slight wind like water.

-Henry David Thoreau
Walden

Caesar's Synonyms

Here are words that are similar to the words in our list, but are they exactly the same in meaning? Or are they slightly different? For each word on our list, look up any synonym that you do not know, then pick one, and carefully explain the difference between it and our word.

vulgar: common, vernacular, in bad taste, indelicate, unrefined, excessive, self-displaying, ostentatious, crude, indecent

traverse: cross, navigate, travel, cover, complete

undulate: wave, heave, slither, sweep, swell, snake, surge, roll, billow, curve, purl, ripple, roll, balloon

vivid: evident, colorful, distinct, noticeable, manifest, obvious, graphic, conspicuous, perceptible, palpable

pallid (adjective form of **pallor**): faded, pale, pasty, wan, white, colorless, ghostly, bleached, ashen, blanched, washed-out

Real Latin
From Juvenal:

Maxima debetur puero reverentia
The greatest respect is owed to a child.

A Wordy Story...

Jane had come aboard with a pallid and melancholy visage, but now, as the white sails filled with wind, and the amiable sea birds clamored with hungry enthusiasm, and the prodigious wooden ship began to traverse the far, undulating sea, her incredulous irritation with the odious details of the vulgar world began to abate, and she sank into a serene repose as she looked over the varnished railing at the vivid and venerable sea, sparkling to the horizon. She looked down at the foam sweeping by, and tried to gaze into the profound depths, but a languor crept over her, and a placid contentment, and she enjoyed the sublime and exquisite happiness that she felt. No longer was she tremulous with unhappiness; indeed, her countenance manifested a singular perplexity.

Caesar's Rewrites

Here are sentences from famous books. In each case, rewrite the sentence into more ordinary words. Example from Marjorie Rawlings's *The Yearling*: "A languor crept over him." The rewrite: Little by little, he began to feel lazy.

From Mark Twain's *Tom Sawyer*: "His mind was **traversing** the whole field of human thought."

From H.G. Wells's *The War of the Worlds*: "[We] scoffed at the **vulgar** idea of [Mars] having inhabitants who were signalling us."

From Stephen Crane's *The Red Badge of Courage*: "His face was of a clammy **pallor**."

From Jean Craighead George's *Julie of the Wolves*: "Their voices **undulated** as each harmonized with the other."

From Kenneth Grahame's *The Wind in the Willows*: "The colours became so **vivid** that with another squeeze they must go on fire."

Caesar's Favorite Word

Think carefully about each of the words in this lesson, and predict which of these Caesar's English words you think you will use most often. Explain why you made this word your choice, and give at least three examples of situations in which you could use that word.

Caesar's Antonyms

For each of the Caesar's English words in this lesson, think of a word that means the opposite. A word that means the opposite is known as an **antonym**.

1. **vulgar**
2. **traverse**
3. **undulate**
4. **vivid**
5. **pallor**

Are there any words in this list that have no antonyms? Are there any that it is very difficult to think of an antonym for? Why?

Caesar's Analogy

Analogies are about relationships. Find a second pair of words that have the same relationship to each other as the first pair has. Remember that it sometimes helps to put the two words into a sentence that makes the relationship clear.

VIVID : PALLID ::

a. visage : countenance
b. melancholy : cheerful
c. undulate : wave
d. venerate : elder

Review for Cumulative Quiz

bi	two	**sub**	under
de	down	**pre**	before
super	over	**un**	not
inter	between	**semi**	half
dis	away	**sym**	together
circum	around	**mal**	bad
post	after	**equi**	equal
ante	before	**aqua**	water
audi	hear	**scrib**	write
cede	go	**cise**	cut
cred	believe	**miss**	send
cide	kill	**dict**	say
bell	war	**spec**	look
pend	hang	**omni**	all
re	again	**ex**	out

countenance	facial expression	**profound**	deep
manifest	obvious	**prodigious**	huge
languor	weakness	**serene**	calm
acute	sharp	**grotesque**	distorted
condescend	to patronize	**odious**	hateful
exquisite	beautifully made	**clamor**	outcry
sublime	lofty	**tremulous**	quivering
allude	indirectly refer to	**placid**	calm
singular	unique	**amiable**	friendly
incredulous	skeptical	**perplex**	confuse
melancholy	sadness	**visage**	the face
venerate	to respect	**abate**	to lessen
repose	resting	**vulgar**	common
traverse	to cross	**undulate**	to wave
vivid	bright	**pallor**	paleness

pallor
paleness

His face was of a clammy pallor.

- Stephen Crane
The Red Badge of Courage

Caesar's English
Ancient Latin Stems
Lesson Thirteen

Latin Stem List

stem	meaning	modern examples
bene	(good)	benefit, benediction, benefactor
son	(sound)	sonorous, dissonance, sonnet
nov	(new)	novice, nova, innovation
sangui	(blood)	sanguine, sanguinary, consanguinity
cogn	(know)	cognizance, incognito, cognoscenti

Latin Stem Talk

BENE means good. A *benefit* is a good thing to receive, a *benediction* is a blessing, and a *benefactor* is a person who does a good thing!

SON means sound. *Sonorous* describes a full, loud sound; *dissonance* is a clashing, harsh sound, and a *sonnet* is a beautiful-sounding fourteen-line poem!

NOV means new. A *novice* is a beginner, a *nova* is a new star, and an *innovation* is a new idea!

SANGUI means blood. *Sanguine* means cheerful, (with rosy, blood-filled cheeks!), *sanguinary* means bloody, and *consanguinity* means related by blood.

COGN means know. *Cognizance* is knowing, *incognito* means in disguise (unknown), and the *cognoscenti* are the people who are said to know best!

Caesar's Analogy

The first two words are related to each other in a special way. Is one before the other? Is one inside the other? Are they opposites? Find the pair below that has the same relationship as the first pair!

NOVICE : PERSON ::

a. nova : star
b. beginner : expert
c. new : old
d. child : adult

Advanced Words: Cognizance

The noun **cognizance** (cog-nih-zance), from the Latin *cognoscere*, contains the stem **cogn** (know) and refers to the condition of awareness, of knowing. In England, they spell *cognizance* and its adjective *cognizant* with an *s*: *cognisant*. In his novel *The American*, Henry James wrote that "He found himself in an atmosphere in which apparently no cognisance was taken of grievances." Martin Luther King once wrote: "I am cognizant of the interrelatedness of all communities and states."

Advanced Word: Sanguine

From the Latin *sanguineus*, meaning bloody, our adjective **sanguine** is one of the oldest of the great words we get from the Romans. Surprisingly, *sanguine* means cheerful, rosy-cheeked, and was used by Chaucer in 1385, in the very beginning of English literature; in his epic poem *The Canterbury Tales*, Chaucer wrote, "His lippes rounde, his colour was sangwyn." Notice the very old spelling of these familiar words. Over five hundred years later, in *The Wind in the Willows*, Kenneth Grahame wrote that "Toad was very much the same sanguine, self-satisfied animal that he had been of old." In *Dracula* Bram Stoker wrote that Renfield had a "Sanguine temperament." James Fennimore Cooper used **sanguine** in *The Last of the Mohicans*; he wrote that "The conviction forced itself on her mind that the too sanguine and generous Duncan had been cruelly deceived."

Which of these examples of **sanguine** do you like the best?

How many different meanings of **sanguine** do you see?

How many of these novels that use **sanguine** have you heard of before?

Who's That Writer?

It is important to notice Geoffrey Chaucer because he helped to establish English literature long ago, in the fourteenth century. Chaucer shows us how old our literature is. Born in London in 1343, Chaucer wrote a masterpiece of poetry, *The Canterbury Tales*. Today it is difficult to read Chaucer because he wrote in an early form of English, with spellings and vocabulary that seem very strange to us, but even in Chaucer's poetry we still see him using great English words like **sanguine** that are important to this day. You will not read Chaucer until perhaps college; his work is difficult and does not have children's themes, but the day will come when a teacher or college professor will assign Chaucer, who has been called the English Homer, and you will see how English literature began, many centuries ago.

Real Latin

Qui naturam sequitur sapiens est.
He who follows nature is wise.

Caesar's Spanish

stem	meaning	English / Spanish examples
bene	(good)	benediction / bendición
son	(sound)	sonorous / sonoro
nov	(new)	novice / novicio
sangui	(blood)	sanguine / sanguíneo
cogn	(know)	cognizance / cognición

A Roman Fact

At their peak, the Roman aqueduct systems brought more than 300,000,000 gallons of fresh water into the city every day.

Caesar's Word Search

In the box below, find the Latin-based English words. They might be vertical, horizontal, or at angles. Circle each word that you find.

```
C S N I N N O V A T I O N C
O A C O G N O S C E N T I O
G N L G V Y G F L E Y P E N
N G P Y T I F X C U N D Q S
I U N O V A C N X O R U S A
Z I F J T Q A E I O O W D N
A N R A O N N T T S U L G
N A B Q O I C C I U T G B U
C R K S U I A N O E U U V I
E Y S G D F G R N S T A J N
X I N E E O O N D K F S G I
D A N N C N O S R U U I T T
S E E N O S O U J P G M B Y
B B I S V B E N E F I T R J
```

__ BENEFIT	__ BENEDICTION	__ BENEFACTOR	__ SONOROUS
__ DISSONANCE	__ SONNET	__ NOVICE	__ NOVA
__ INNOVATION	__ SANGUINE	__ SANGUINARY	__ CONSANGUINITY
__ COGNIZANCE	__ INCOGNITO	__ COGNOSCENTI	

Julius Caesar, from his *Commentaries on the Gallic Wars*:

Caesar got a Gallic horseman to take a letter about his plans to Cicero, which he wrote in Greek for fear of interception. If the Gaul was unable to get into Cicero's camp, he was to tie the letter to a javelin thong, and throw it over the rampart. The letter said, "Caesar is coming; fight."

Review for Cumulative Quiz

bi	two	**sub**	under
de	down	**pre**	before
super	over	**un**	not
inter	between	**semi**	half
dis	away	**sym**	together
circum	around	**mal**	bad
post	after	**equi**	equal
ante	before	**aqua**	water
audi	hear	**scrib**	write
cede	go	**cise**	cut
cred	believe	**miss**	send
cide	kill	**dict**	say
bell	war	**spec**	look
pend	hang	**omni**	all
re	again	**ex**	out
bene	good	**son**	sound
nov	new	**sangui**	blood
cogn	know		

countenance	facial expression	**profound**	deep
manifest	obvious	**prodigious**	huge
languor	weakness	**serene**	calm
acute	sharp	**grotesque**	distorted
condescend	to patronize	**odious**	hateful
exquisite	beautifully made	**clamor**	outcry
sublime	lofty	**tremulous**	quivering
allude	indirectly refer to	**placid**	calm
singular	unique	**amiable**	friendly
incredulous	skeptical	**perplex**	confuse
melancholy	sadness	**visage**	the face
venerate	to respect	**abate**	to lessen
repose	resting	**vulgar**	common
traverse	to cross	**undulate**	to wave
vivid	bright	**pallor**	paleness

There are occasions when it is undoubtedly better to incur loss than to make gain.

-Plautus
254 - 184 B.C.

Caesar's English
Vocabulary from Latin
Lesson Fourteen

1. **wistful**: yearning
2. **subtle**: slight
3. **sagacity**: wisdom
4. **remonstrate**: to object
5. **tedious**: boring

wistful

The English adjective **wistful** has a most interesting origin. An example of a great English word that is *not* from Latin, *wistful* traces back to *whist*, which used to be a sound people made when they wanted silence, like *shhh* or *shush*. In other words wistful is an example of onomatopoeia, a word that sounds like a sound! **Wistful** was used by Jonathan Swift in his 1726 book *Gulliver's Travels*, where there was "many a wistful melancholy look towards the sea." In Sir Walter Scott's 1820 novel of knighthood, *Ivanhoe*, "The hermit cast a wistful look upon the knight." In Mark Twain's *Tom Sawyer*, we read that "It was discomforting to see Huck eyeing Joe's preparations so wistfully." In his great novel of dogs and wolves in the far north, *The Call of the Wild*, Jack London wrote that "Charles looked on wistfully." Can a plant be wistful? Well, Kenneth Grahame, in *The Wind in the Willows*, described "Willow-herb, tender and wistful." Why do you think Grahame chose this adjective to describe the willow-herb? In Frances Hodgson Burnett's *The Secret Garden*, written in 1911, we read "'Could I ever get there?' asked Mary wistfully, looking through her window at the far-off blue." In George Orwell's *Animal Farm*,

"Wistful glances were sent in the direction of Foxwood." If someone had a wistful expression on his face, what would it look like?

Can you tell that **wistful** does not sound Latin? What do you notice about the music of the Latin words, that is different from this word?

subtle

The adjective **subtle** is one of the oldest words in the English language. Although it can be traced back to the Latin *subtilis*, where it meant the same thing as it does today, it was already in use as an English word in 1385, when Chaucer wrote *The Canterbury Tales*. Chaucer wrote, "And two of us shul kepen subtilly This tresor wel" —Two of us shall keep subtly this treasure well. They certainly spelled things differently over 600 years ago! In H.G. Wells's *The War of the Worlds*, a character describes the Martian fighting machines: "He presented them as tilted, stiff tripods, without either flexibility or subtlety." Actually, the Martian fighting machines, even though they were made of metal, were swift and agile, and capable of subtle movements and actions. James Barrie used **subtle** in *Peter Pan* to describe a "subtle mind." In his 1908 novel of animal characters living by the river, *The Wind in the Willows*, Kenneth Grahame described "the more subtle of the physical senses."

In 1895, Stephen Crane wrote one of the great war novels of American literature; called *The Red Badge of Courage*, Crane's novel was so realistic that Civil War veterans thought he had witnessed the war. Actually, he wasn't even born when the war took place. The novel is the story of a young boy who goes off to fight for the Union. Dreaming of being a hero, he instead grows up, and longs at the end not for war but for peace, soft and eternal peace. In *The Red Badge of Courage*, the young boy receives a "subtle suggestion to touch the corpse."

sagacity

The English noun **sagacity** comes from the Latin *sagax*, wise. From *sagax* came the Latin *sagacitas*, and eventually, our English word **sagacity**. When someone has sagacity, they are **sagacious**—they have sound judgment and a keen mind. When someone is like that, we call them a **sage**. In Jonathan Swift's *Gulliver's Travels*, someone is described as "below the sagacity of a common hound"! Swift also observed that "among other animals, bees and ants had the reputation of more industry, art, and sagacity than many of the larger kinds." Why do you think Swift called bees and ants sagacious? Author Mary Shelley's poor pitiful *Frankenstein* monster said of himself, "I had sagacity enough to discover, that the unnatural hideousness of my person was the chief object of horror with those who had formerly beheld me." Sir Walter Scott wrote about the wisdom of horses! In *Ivanhoe*, Scott wrote that "the knight resolved to trust to the sagacity of his horse." In what way do you think a horse could have sagacity? Guess what animal James Fennimore Cooper called **sagacious** in *The Last of the Mohicans*? A bear! Cooper wrote of "that air of sagacity that a bear is known to possess." After running from the battlefield in panic, Stephen Crane's hero Henry Fleming in *The Red Badge of Courage* tried to convince himself that "His actions had been sagacious things."

remonstrate

To **remonstrate** is to plead in protest, to argue repeatedly over something. The word comes from the Latin *remonstrare*, with *re* meaning again and *monstrare* meaning to show. When you remonstrate, that is **remonstrance**. Characters in novels are always remonstrating, since life is so upsetting at times. In *Ivanhoe*, Scott wrote that "The Saxon, indeed, had remonstrated strongly with his friend upon the injudicious choice he had made of his party." In Harriet Beecher

Stowe's great novel, *Uncle Tom's Cabin*, which was an attack against the inhumanity of slavery, we read that "A nation has a right to argue, remonstrate, implore." In George Eliot's book *Silas Marner*, a dog, Snap, remonstrates with a cat! We find "Snap occasionally desisting in order to remonstrate with the cat by a cogent worrying growl on the greediness and futility of her conduct." George Eliot, one of the great writers of British literature, was actually a woman, Mary Ann Evans. She led an unusual life, and many people in England rejected her. One good example of **remonstrate** comes in James M. Barrie's *Peter Pan*: "'Wendy,' remonstrated Michael, 'I'm too big for a cradle.'" Do you see how Michael is pleading in protest against having to sleep in a cradle?

tedious

The English adjective **tedious** traces back to the Latin adjective *taedios* and the Latin noun *taedium*. **Tedious** means dull, boring, tiresome. A long, uninteresting lecture would be tedious. When someone keeps giving you long instructions after you already understand what to do, that is tedious. Interestingly, **tedious** was one of William Shakespeare's favorite words. He used it over and over again in his plays, which were written in the late 1500s and the early 1600s. In *Hamlet*, Shakespeare described "tedious old fools," and the "tedious day." In *Much Ado about Nothing*, one of Shakespeare's characters says, "Neighbors, you are tedious," and wonders about being "as tedious as a King." In *As You Like It*, a character asks, "O most gentle Jupiter, what tedious homily of love have you wearied your parishioners withal?" This means, roughly, What boring love story have you told everybody? Shakespeare also used **tedious** in *Romeo and Juliet*; he wrote, "So tedious is this day," and described "a tedious tale." In *A Midsummer Night's Dream*, we read "I do repent the tedious minutes I with her have spent," "O long and tedious night, abate thy hours!" and then a description of "A tedious brief scene."

Real Latin

Justitia numquam nocet cuiquam.
Justice never harms anybody.

What Is This Writer Saying?
Discuss the meaning of the **bold** word in each of the following sentences:

From Marjorie Kennan Rawlings's *The Yearling*: "The **tedious** hauling would have to be done all over again."

From Washington Irving's *The Legend of Sleepy Hollow*: "With what **wistful** look did he eye every trembling ray of light streaming across the waste fields from some distant window."

From Harriet Beecher Stowe's *Uncle Tom's Cabin*: "So **subtle** is the atmosphere of opinion, that it will make itself felt, without words."

From Herman Melville's *Moby Dick*: "Does the ocean furnish any fish that in disposition answers to the **sagacious** kindness of the dog?"

From Bram Stoker's *Dracula*: "Van Helsing had a way of going on his own road, no matter who **remonstrated**."

sagacity
wisdom

The knight resolved to trust to the sagacity of his horse.

-Sir Walter Scott
Ivanhoe

Caesar's Synonyms

Here are words that are similar to the words in our list, but are they exactly the same in meaning? Or are they slightly different? For each word on our list, look up any synonym that you do not know, then pick one, and carefully explain the difference between it and our word.

wistful: melancholy, sad, longing, pensive, sentimental, yearning, homesick, nostalgic

subtle: slight, elusive, abstruse, delicate

sagacity: insight, wisdom, sapience, acumen, understanding, perspicacity, vision, depth, profundity, perception

remonstrate: protest, object, expostulate, complain, reprove

tedious: boring, dull, slow, tiresome

Caesar's Rewrites

Here are some sentences from famous books. In each case, rewrite the sentence into more ordinary words. Example from Marjorie Rawlings's *The Yearling*: "A languor crept over him." The rewrite: Little by little, he began to feel lazy.

From Marjorie Rawlings's *The Yearling*: "If Fodder-wing had been alive, Jody thought **wistfully**, the two of them might have been taken along to Jacksonville."

From James M. Barrie's *Peter Pan*: "'Wendy,' **remonstrated** Michael, 'I'm too big for a cradle.'"

From Frederick Douglass's *The Narrative of Frederick Douglass*: "Thus, after a long **tedious** effort for years, I finally succeeded in learning how to write."

From James Fennimore Cooper's *The Last of the Mohicans*: "The two parties began to prepare themselves for a **subtle** trial of their wits."

From Sir Walter Scott's *Ivanhoe*: "The knight resolved to trust to the **sagacity** of his horse."

Caesar's Favorite Word

Think carefully about each of the words in this lesson, and predict which of these Caesar's English words you think you will use most often. Explain why you made this word your choice, and give at least three examples of situations in which you could use that word.

Carsar's Antonyms

For each of the Caesar's English words in this lesson, think of a word that means the opposite. A word that means the opposite is known as an **antonym**.

1. **wistful**
2. **subtle**
3. **sagacity**
4. **remonstrate**
5. **tedious**

Are there any words in this list that have no antonyms? Are there any that it is very difficult to think of an antonym for? Why?

Caesar's Spanish

Everywhere we turn, language reveals to us that modern English and modern Spanish are both descendants of ancient Latin:

Latin	*Spanish*	*English*
subtilis	sutile	subtle
sagacitas	sagacidad	sagacity
taediosus	tedioso	tedious

Caesar's Analogies

Analogies are about relationships. Find a second pair of words that have the same relationship to each other as the first pair has. Remember that it sometimes helps to put the two words into a sentence that makes the relationship clear.

SAGACIOUS : PROPHET ::
   a. verbal : writer
   b. victim : martyr
   c. prostrate : upright
   d. articulate : mute

REMONSTRATE : AGREE ::
   a. sagacity : wisdom
   b. abyss : ocean
   c. subtle : obvious
   d. vex : irritate

Review for Cumulative Quiz

bi	two	**sub**	under
de	down	**pre**	before
super	over	**un**	not
inter	between	**semi**	half
dis	away	**sym**	together
circum	around	**mal**	bad
post	after	**equi**	equal
ante	before	**aqua**	water
audi	hear	**scrib**	write
cede	go	**cise**	cut
cred	believe	**miss**	send
cide	kill	**dict**	say
bell	war	**spec**	look
pend	hang	**omni**	all
re	again	**ex**	out
bene	good	**son**	sound
nov	new	**sangui**	blood
cogn	know		

countenance	facial expression	**profound**	deep
manifest	obvious	**prodigious**	huge
languor	weakness	**serene**	calm
acute	sharp	**grotesque**	distorted
condescend	to patronize	**odious**	hateful
exquisite	beautifully made	**clamor**	outcry
sublime	lofty	**tremulous**	quivering
allude	indirectly refer to	**placid**	calm
singular	unique	**amiable**	friendly
incredulous	skeptical	**perplex**	confuse
melancholy	sadness	**visage**	the face
venerate	to respect	**abate**	to lessen
repose	resting	**wistful**	yearning
subtle	slight	**sagacity**	wisdom
remonstrate	to object	**tedious**	boring
vulgar	common	**traverse**	to cross
undulate	to wave	**vivid**	bright
pallor	paleness		

tedious
boring

It would be tedious
to trouble the reader
with relating the
vast numbers.

-Jonathan Swift
Gulliver's Travels

138   138

Caesar's English
Ancient Latin Stems
Lesson Fifteen

Latin Stem List

stem	meaning	modern examples
ject	(throw)	dejection, interject, conjecture
dorm	(sleep)	dormant, dormitory, dormer
magn	(great)	magnate, magnificent, magnanimous
ver	(true)	verify, veracity, verdict
put	(think)	dispute, putative, reputation

Latin Stem Talk

JECT means throw. *Dejection* means feeling down, to *interject* is to interrupt, and a *conjecture* is a guess!

DORM means sleep. *Dormant* means asleep, a *dormitory* is a building that houses students and gives them a place to sleep, and *dormer* windows stick out of the upper floor of a building, where the bedrooms are!

MAGN means great. *Magnificent* means great, a *magnate* is a great or powerful person, and *magnanimous* refers to greatness or generosity of mind!

VER means true. To *verify* something is to check it to see if it is true, *veracity* is truthfulness, and a *verdict* is the jury's decision of truth in a trial!

PUT (pronounced pyoot) means think. A *dispute* is an argument between people who think differently from each other, *putative* means thought-to-be, and your *reputation* is what other people think of you!

Caesar's Analogy

The first two words are related to each other in a special way. Is one before the other? Is one inside the other? Are they opposites? Find the pair below that has the same relationship as the first pair!

DEJECTION : MOOD ::
   a. dispute : agreement
   b. verdict : decision
   c. magnanimous : small-minded
   d. verify : report

Advanced Word: Magnanimous

The adjective **magnanimous** comes from the stems *magn*, great, and *anim*, mind. To be magnanimous is to be generous, noble in one's thoughts. The noun form of the word is *magnanimity*. In Jonathan Swift's *Gulliver's Travels* there is a "magnanimous prince," and in Stowe's *Uncle Tom's Cabin* we read about "that natural magnanimity and generosity of mind which one often marks as characteristic of the women of Kentucky."

Advanced Word: Dejection

The English noun **dejection**, or its adjective form *dejected*, has been popular in English literature since the time of Shakespeare. *Dejection* comes from the Latin *dejectio*, a throwing down; dejection is when we are thrown (ject) down (de) in spirit, sad, and full of despair. In Defoe's 1719 novel *Robinson Crusoe*, he wrote that "All this while I sat upon the ground very much terrified and dejected." In Sir Walter Scott's *Ivanhoe*, we find that "Her demeanor was serious, but not dejected." Harriet Beecher Stowe wrote that "the whole gang sat with downcast, dejected faces." "Hook was profoundly dejected" in Barrie's *Peter Pan*, and Barrie wrote that "He was roused from this dejection by Smee's eager voice." Stephen Crane wrote in *The Red Badge of Courage* that "Their smudged countenances now expressed a profound dejection." In Grahame's *The Wind in the Willows* there is a "limp and dejected Toad," and we learn that "the Mole, limp and dejected, took his seat in the stern of the boat." And in John Steinbeck's *Of Mice and Men*, "Lennie sat down on the ground and hung his head dejectedly."

Which of these examples of **dejection** do you like the best?

How many different meanings of **dejection** do you see?

How many of these novels that use **dejection** have you heard of before?

Who's That Writer?

Harriet Beecher Stowe was an abolitionist—someone who wanted to abolish slavery. Her great novel, *Uncle Tom's Cabin*, was intended to enrage all who read it against the horrible cruelty of slavery. She was born in Litchfield, Connecticut, in 1811, the daughter of a liberal clergyman. When *Uncle Tom's Cabin* was published in 1852, it created a storm; it sold 500,000 copies in the U.S. in the first five years and was translated into twenty languages. Stowe died in 1896.

Caesar's Spanish

stem	meaning	English / Spanish examples
ject	(throw)	interjection / interjección
dorm	(sleep)	dormant / durmiente
magn	(great)	magnanimous / magnánimo
ver	(true)	verify / verificar
put	(think)	dispute / disputar

A Roman Fact

The Roman Stoic philosophers taught that in order to acquire wisdom we should read the philosophers, not once but repeatedly, and that we should read the original works in depth, not just the summaries. "Give over hoping," they said "that you can skim, by means of epitomes, the wisdom of distinguished men."

Caesar's Word Search

In the box below, find the Latin-based English words. They might be vertical, horizontal, or at angles. Circle each word that you find.

```
N O I K P U T A T I V E L A
U D V R E P U T A T I O N D
V V E F E C S T N T K R M O
E E R J D B O R C E D T A R
R R A B E X G E R Z N D G M
I D C E T C J U L E E O N I
F I I V M R T B C T P R A T
Y C T Y E C R I A K E M N O
S T Y T E E F N O T Z A I R
U P N J M I G J U N Y N M Y
E I N R N A L P R T F T O L
X O O G M U S J P T P K U K
C D A K F I Y V A P U S S S
M M T L D J Q J T Y G R W Z
```

_ DEJECTION   _ INTERJECT   _ CONJECTURE   _ DORMANT
_ DORMITORY   _ DORMER   _ MAGNATE   _ MAGNIFICENT
_ MAGNANIMOUS   _ VERIFY   _ VERACITY   _ VERDICT
_ DISPUTE   _ PUTATIVE   _ REPUTATION

Julius Caesar, from his *Commentaries on the Gallic Wars*:

On receiving his dispatch, Caesar sent a rider to Marcus Crassus, twenty-four miles away, commanding him to march his legion at midnight and come with great haste.

Continual dropping wears away a stone.

- Lucretius
95 - 55 B.C.

Real Latin
From Ovid:

Caeser aeduis obsides imperat.
Caeser demanded hostages of the Aedui.

Review for Cumulative Quiz

bi	two	**sub**	under
de	down	**pre**	before
super	over	**un**	not
inter	between	**semi**	half
dis	away	**sym**	together
circum	around	**mal**	bad
post	after	**equi**	equal
ante	before	**aqua**	water
audi	hear	**scrib**	write
cede	go	**cise**	cut
cred	believe	**miss**	send
cide	kill	**dict**	say
bell	war	**spec**	look
pend	hang	**omni**	all
re	again	**ex**	out
bene	good	**son**	sound
nov	new	**sangui**	blood
cogn	know	**ject**	throw
dorm	sleep	**magn**	great
ver	true	**put**	think

countenance	facial expression	**profound**	deep
manifest	obvious	**prodigious**	huge
languor	weakness	**serene**	calm
acute	sharp	**grotesque**	distorted
condescend	to patronize	**odious**	hateful
exquisite	beautifully made	**clamor**	outcry
sublime	lofty	**tremulous**	quivering
allude	indirectly refer to	**placid**	calm
singular	unique	**amiable**	friendly
incredulous	skeptical	**perplex**	confuse
melancholy	sadness	**visage**	the face
venerate	to respect	**abate**	to lessen
repose	resting	**wistful**	yearning
subtle	slight	**sagacity**	wisdom
remonstrate	to object	**tedious**	boring
vulgar	common	**traverse**	to cross
undulate	to wave	**vivid**	bright
pallor	paleness		

Caesar's English
Vocabulary from Latin
Lesson Sixteen

1. **articulate**: express clearly
2. **vex**: to irritate
3. **prostrate**: lying down
4. **abyss**: a bottomless depth
5. **martyr**: one who suffers

articulate

The English word **articulate** is sometimes a verb, pronounced arr-tick-you-late. We articulate the feelings we have inside us. The word is also used as an adjective to modify nouns or pronouns, and then it is pronounced *arr-tick-you-laht*. We might say that Thomas Jefferson was an articulate man. Curiously, **articulate** comes from the Latin word *articulatus*, which meant distinct or jointed. Even today, we talk about articulated joints in insect legs. What do joints have to do with being capable of speech or of speaking very clearly? The idea is that a good speaker can JOIN all of the words together in the right way. A less articulate speaker puts words in the wrong places, or even uses the wrong words, and so is unclear. When you can't express yourself, you are **inarticulate**. In Kenneth Grahame's *The Wind in the Willows*, there is "a sudden clear call from an actual articulate voice." Jack London, in *The Call of the Wild*, described "a cry that was inarticulate and more like the cry of an animal." In *The War of the Worlds*, H.G. Well writes that "It was scarcely a time for articulate conversation." Once in a while, **articulate** refers to real joints, not just speech. For example, in Bram Stoker's famous novel *Dracula* we read that "The Castle of Dracula now stood out against the red sky and every stone of its broken battlements was articulated against the light of the setting sun."

vex

Our English verb **vex** means to irritate, bother, or baffle. If you annoy or provoke people, you are vexing them. If you trouble people, worry them, or torment them, you are vexing them. The condition of being vexed is **vexation**. Something that vexes you is **vexatious**. **Vex**, like almost all of the great words we use, comes from the Romans. The Latin *vexare* meant to shake, jolt, or annoy. Emotionally speaking, an upsetting thing shakes you up. In Shakespeare's 1594 play *The Taming of the Shrew*, we read that "such an injury would vex a very saint." In Sir Walter Scott's *Ivanhoe*, there is "the laughter of his companions, who, as usual in such cases, enjoyed his vexation." In *Tom Sawyer*, Mark Twain wrote that "Aunt Polly was vexed to think she had overlooked that bit of circumstantial evidence." Frances Hodgson Burnett used **vex** in *The Secret Garden*: "You needn't be so vexed." In Barrie's *Peter Pan*, there is an effort "to vex her still more." And in Stephen Crane's *The Red Badge of Courage*, "His face was dark with vexation and wrath." In Lewis Carroll's *Alice in Wonderland*, we see the knight with "a shade of vexation passing over his face." At another point, "Alice stood looking after it, almost ready to cry with vexation at having lost her dear little fellow-traveler so suddenly." It is vexing to think how many ways we can use **vex**; the great authors certainly use it a lot.

prostrate

Our English word **prostrate** comes from the Latin *prosternere*, which meant to throw prone. What does "throw prone" mean? It means to throw yourself down flat on the ground, so you are lying face-down. **Prostrate** is sometimes a verb; you can prostrate yourself. Sometimes, **prostrate** is an adjective: we might say that a person was prostrate and trembling on the ground. Usually, falling prostrate is a sign of submission or humiliation. You might prostrate yourself before an Emperor. In Shakespeare's *Romeo and Juliet*, a character is urged "to fall prostrate here." In Jonathan Swift's *Gulliver's Travels*, Gulliver encounters horse-like creatures, and says that "I was going to prostrate myself to kiss his hoof." In *Ivanhoe*, Sir Walter Scott writes that "The lion preys not on prostrate carcasses." James M. Barrie used **prostrate** in *Peter Pan*: "They called Peter the Great White Father, prostrating themselves before him." We also see it in Kenneth Grahame's *The Wind in the Willows*: "He found himself lying on top of the prostrate Rat." In Natalie Babbitt's novel *Tuck Everlasting*, we learn that "she told the prostrate group in the parlor."

abyss

The English noun **abyss** does come to us from the Latin *abyssus*, but in this case, the Romans got it from the ancient Greeks, whose word *abyssos* meant bottomless. Today in our language it means the same thing still; an abyss—pronounced ah-BISS with the stress on the second syllable—is a bottomless depth. Sometimes we talk about the abysses in the oceans, and sometimes we make a poetic comparison and call the universe an abyss. We could call the Grand Canyon an abyss. In Sir Walter Scott's *Ivanhoe* there is "an abyss of infamy." If an idea is really deep, we might even call that an abyss. In Bonner's translation of Jules Verne's *20,000 Leagues Under the Sea*, we read that "the Nautilus was following it down into the abyss" and that "one's first thoughts are about the abyss below." In Marjorie Rawlings's *The Yearling*, she writes that "It was as though it were blowing in another world, across a dark abyss." In James Fennimore Cooper's *The Last of the Mohicans*, hoarser yells "arose out of the abyss of the deep ravine."

martyr

A **martyr** is someone who suffers or dies for a principle. The word actually traces back through Latin *martyr* to the Greek *martys*, a witness. In Jules Verne's *20,000 Leagues Under the Sea*, the question is asked about Captain Nemo, who was using the Nautilus to sink warships: "Was he a martyr or executioner?" In Bram Stoker's *Dracula*, we read that "Her eyes shone with the devotion of a martyr."

What is This Writer Saying?

Discuss the meaning of the **bold** word in each of the following sentences:

From Emily Bronte's *Jane Eyre*: "I sank **prostrate** with my face to the ground."

From William Golding's *Lord of the Flies*: There was "a harsh cry that seemed to come out of the **abyss** of ages."

From H.G. Wells's *The War of the Worlds*: "He came sliding down the rubbish and crept beside me in the darkness, **inarticulate**, gesticulating."

From William Thackeray's *Vanity Fair*: "He felt that he was a **martyr** to duty."

From Lewis Carroll's *Alice in Wonderland*: "Alice stood looking after it, almost ready to cry with **vexation** at having lost her dear little fellow-traveler so suddenly."

abyss
a bottomless depth

A harsh cry
seemed to come
out of the abyss of ages.

-William Golding
Lord of the Flies

Caesar's Synonyms

Here are words that are similar to the words in our list, but are they exactly the same in meaning? Or are they slightly different? For each word on our list, look up any synonym that you do not know, then pick one, and carefully explain the difference between it and our word.

articulate: expressive, fluent, eloquent, intelligible, enunciated, pronounced

vex: worry, bother, baffle, dismay, fluster, distress, disturb, upset, affront, offend, disgruntle, irritate

prostrate: prone, reclined, repose, lie down, overwhelmed, dropped, felled, crushed, overcome

abyss: bottomless depth, pit, chasm, gulf, gorge, crater, gulch

martyr: one who is: abused, victimized, subjugated, tormented, wronged, persecuted, mistreated, harmed, oppressed, afflicted

Real Latin
From Ovid:

Rident stolidi verba Latina.
Fools laugh at the Latin language.

Julius Caesar, from his *Commentaries on the Gallic Wars*:

Caesar laid roads across the marsh and led his legions to the hill. Reforming his soldiers, he drew up his battle line in front of the close-packed Gauls, where they were in range of his artillery.

A Wordy Story...

A subtle breeze blew from the undulating sea as Ishmael lay prostrate on the beach. The sagacity within him remonstrated with another part of him to get up and get back to work, but he was vexed with the tedious repetition of his job, and he stared out over the blue abyss, wistfully remembering his days as a sailor. He could not really articulate to himself why he wanted to return to the sea, with its prodigious storms and manifest dangers, but his countenance grew serene as he saw vivid images in his mind, images of martyrs to the seafaring life, images of grotesque old sailors in seaports, images of amiable people, and odious people, and sublime experiences. Suddenly, these exquisite thoughts became too acute, and clamored in his mind, and he turned his visage back to the stiff sea wind as the memories began to abate. He knew, though, that he would always venerate the great experiences he had known, even on a day of placid repose, like this one.

Caesar's Rewrites

Here are some sentences from famous books. In each case, rewrite the sentence into more ordinary words. Example from Marjorie Rawlings's *The Yearling*: "A languor crept over him." The rewrite: Little by little, he began to feel lazy.

From Jonathan Swift's *Gulliver's Travels*: "I made my acknowledgments by **prostrating** myself at his Majesty's feet."

From Stephen Crane's *The Red Badge of Courage:* "His face was dark with **vexation** and wrath."

From Rudyard Kipling's *Kim*: "The old man groaned, **inarticulate** with amazement."

From H.G. Wells's *The Time Machine*: "Their eyes were abnormally large and sensitive, just as the pupils of the **abysmal** fishes."

From Bram Stoker's *Dracula*: "Her eyes shone with the devotion of a **martyr**."

Caesar's Favorite Word

Think carefully about each of the words in this lesson, and predict which of these Caesar's English words you think you will use most often. Explain why you made this word your choice, and give at least three examples of situations in which you could use that word.

Caesar's Antonyms

For each of the Caesar's English words in this lesson, think of a word that means the opposite.

1. **articulate**
2. **vex**
3. **prostrate**
4. **abyss**
5. **martyr**

Are there any words in this list that have no antonyms? Are there any that it is very difficult to think of an antonym for? Why?

Caesar's Analogy

Analogies are about relationships. Find a second pair of words that have the same relationship to each other as the first pair has. Remember that it sometimes helps to put the two words into a sentence that makes the relationship clear.

VEX : IRRITATE ::
  a. tedious : lecture
  b. articulate : speak
  c. sagacity : dullness
  d. subtle : change

Caesar's Spanish

Everywhere we turn, language reveals to us that modern English and modern Spanish are both descendants of ancient Latin:

Latin	*Spanish*	*English*
articulatus	articulado	articulate
vexare	vejar	vex
prostratus	postrado	prostrate
abyssus	abismo	abyss
martyr	mártir	martyr

The Pantheon, built to honor all (pan) gods (theo).

Review for Cumulative Quiz

bi	two	**sub**	under
de	down	**pre**	before
super	over	**un**	not
inter	between	**semi**	half
dis	away	**sym**	together
circum	around	**mal**	bad
post	after	**equi**	equal
ante	before	**aqua**	water
audi	hear	**scrib**	write
cede	go	**cise**	cut
cred	believe	**miss**	send
cide	kill	**dict**	say
bell	war	**spec**	look
pend	hang	**omni**	all
re	again	**ex**	out
bene	good	**son**	sound
nov	new	**sangui**	blood
cogn	know	**ject**	throw
dorm	sleep	**magn**	great
ver	true	**put**	think

countenance	facial expression	**profound**	deep
manifest	obvious	**prodigious**	huge
languor	weakness	**serene**	calm
acute	sharp	**grotesque**	distorted
condescend	to patronize	**odious**	hateful
exquisite	beautifully made	**clamor**	outcry
sublime	lofty	**tremulous**	quivering
allude	indirectly refer to	**placid**	calm
singular	unique	**amiable**	friendly
incredulous	skeptical	**perplex**	confuse
melancholy	sadness	**visage**	the face
venerate	to respect	**abate**	to lessen
repose	resting	**wistful**	yearning
subtle	slight	**sagacity**	wisdom
remonstrate	to object	**tedious**	boring
articulate	express clearly	**vex**	to irritate
prostrate	lying down	**abyss**	bottomless depth
martyr	one who suffers	**vulgar**	common
traverse	to cross	**undulate**	to wave
vivid	bright	**pallor**	paleness

martyr
one who suffers for a cause

There are some men
who long for martyrdom.

-Alan Paton
Cry, the Beloved Country

Caesar's English
Ancient Latin Stems
Lesson Seventeen

Five Stems of Greek Origin:

stem	meaning	modern examples
archy	(government)	monarchy, oligarchy, anarchy
bio	(life)	biology, biography, biomorphic
auto	(self)	autograph, autocracy, autobiography
chron	(time)	chronic, chronological, synchronize
dec	(ten)	decade, decimal, decimate

Latin Stem Talk

ARCHY means government. A *monarchy* is a government of one person, like a king; an *oligarchy* is a government of a few people, and *anarchy* is the lawless lack of government!

BIO means life. *Biology* is the study of living things; a *biography* is a book telling about the life of a person, and *biomorphic* sculpture has rounded and curving shapes in it that resemble the forms found in nature!

AUTO means self. In an *autograph*, you write your own name; an *autocracy* is a government like a monarchy where the ruler can make all decisions himself, and an *autobiography* is a book you write telling the story of your own life!

CHRON means time. A *chronic* cold is one that lasts a long time; *chronological* means in time-order from past to present, and to *synchronize* watches means to set them to the same time!

DEC means ten. A *decade* is ten years; the *decimal* system is a number system based on tens, and a *decimated* army has lost ten percent or more of its soldiers!

Caesar's Analogy

The first two words are related to each other in a special way. Is one before the other? Is one inside the other? Are they opposites? Find the pair below that has the same relationship as the first pair!

BIOGRAPHY : CHRONOLOGICAL ::
a. chronic : brief
b. autograph : signature
c. autocracy : monarchy
d. counting : sequential

Advanced Word: Anarchy

The noun **anarchy** (ANN-ark-ee) contains the stem **an**, not, and **archy**, government. From the Latin *anarchia*, which came from the Greek *anarchios*, leaderless, **anarchy** is when there is no government, perhaps because the former government has fallen, and different groups are struggling for power. Anarchy can also be any disordered, uncontrolled condition. In *Why We Can't Wait*, Dr. Martin Luther King wrote that "we were not anarchists advocating lawlessness."

Advanced Word: Chronic

The adjective **chronic**, from the Latin *chronicus* which came from the Greek *chronikos*, means lasting or happening frequently, and it has been used by many writers in the last two centuries. In *Uncle Tom's Cabin* Harriet Beecher Stowe wrote that "A sort of chronic remorse went with him everywhere." Herman Melville, in *Moby Dick*, described a "chronically broken back." In *The American*, Henry James wrote that "It made him chronically uncomfortable," and in *Tom Sawyer*, Mark Twain wrote that "The dreadful secret of the murder was a chronic misery." In *The Call of the Wild*, Jack London described the outside dogs, "whose digestions had not been trained by chronic famine to make the most of little." Rachel Carson, in her environmental classic *Silent Spring*, wrote of "a chronic form of leukemia."

Which of these examples of **chronic** do you like the best?

How many different meanings of **chronic** do you see?

How many of these novels that use **chronic** have you heard of before?

Who's That Writer?

Rachel Louise Carson was born in Springdale, Pennsylvania, in 1907. She attended the Pennsylvania College for Women and Johns Hopkins University, and taught zoology at the University of Maryland. She was the first female biologist at the U.S. Bureau of Fisheries and the Fish and Wildlife Service. Her book *The Sea Around Us* won the National Book Award for nonfiction in 1952, but it was her masterpiece, *Silent Spring*, that established her reputation for all time. *Silent Spring* showed the American public the dangers of pesticides, especially of DDT, and resulted in landmark legislation to make the environment a safer place.

Caesar's Spanish

stem	meaning	English / Spanish examples
archy	(government)	monarchy / monarquía
bio	(life)	biology / biología
auto	(self)	autocracy / autocracia
chron	(time)	chronic / crónico
dec	(ten)	decade / década

A Roman Fact

The emperor Caligula, seen on a Roman coin below, loved horse racing, and once gave a charioteer a prize of two million sesterces (Roman money)! He was so devoted to his race horse, Incitatus, that he had a marble stall and ivory manger built for it. Once, he invited the horse to dinner, and even suggested that he would make it a consul!

Real Latin

Video quid facias.
I see what you are doing.

Caesar's Word Search

In the box below, find the Latin-based English words. They might be vertical, horizontal, or at angles. Circle each word that you find

```
A B N T B I O L O G Y B J C
U R I W N M W B P J S I B H
T M O N A R C H Y S Y O I R
O G H A B P J V X C N G O O
B Y V D D I C P A H C R M N
I C P U K E I R R R H A O O
O H A N A R C H Y P R P R L
G R Y H I O L A A F O H P O
R O F F T A C R D J N Y H G
A N B U M O G N B E I K I I
P I A I T O O R C T Z K C C
H C C M T L B X L V E D M A
Y E T U O L I G A R C H Y L
D J A D E C I M A T E Z V Y
```

__ MONARCHY   __ OLIGARCHY   __ ANARCHY   __ BIOLOGY
__ BIOGRAPHY   __ BIOMORPHIC   __ AUTOGRAPH   __ AUTOCRACY
__ AUTOBIOGRAPHY   __ CHRONIC   __ CHRONOLOGICAL __ SYNCHRONIZE
__ DECADE   __ DECIMAL   __ DECIMATE

Julius Caesar, from his *Commentaries on the Gallic Wars*:

Filling their barrels with tallow, pitch, and lath, the enemy set them on fire and hurled them down on us, fiercely attacking at the same time. Our soldiers were unable to fight the enemy and the flames at the same time.

Review for Cumulative Quiz

bi	two	**sub**	under
de	down	**pre**	before
super	over	**un**	not
inter	between	**semi**	half
dis	away	**sym**	together
circum	around	**mal**	bad
post	after	**equi**	equal
ante	before	**aqua**	water
audi	hear	**scrib**	write
cede	go	**cise**	cut
cred	believe	**miss**	send
cide	kill	**dict**	say
bell	war	**spec**	look
pend	hang	**omni**	all
re	again	**ex**	out
bene	good	**son**	sound
nov	new	**sangui**	blood
cogn	know	**ject**	throw
dorm	sleep	**magn**	great
ver	true	**put**	think
archy	government	**bio**	life
auto	self	**chron**	time
dec	ten		

countenance	facial expression	**profound**	deep
manifest	obvious	**prodigious**	huge
languor	weakness	**serene**	calm
acute	sharp	**grotesque**	distorted
condescend	to patronize	**odious**	hateful
exquisite	beautifully made	**clamor**	outcry
sublime	lofty	**tremulous**	quivering
allude	indirectly refer to	**placid**	calm
singular	unique	**amiable**	friendly
incredulous	skeptical	**perplex**	confuse
melancholy	sadness	**visage**	the face
venerate	to respect	**abate**	to lessen
repose	resting	**wistful**	yearning
subtle	slight	**sagacity**	wisdom
remonstrate	to object	**tedious**	boring
articulate	express clearly	**vex**	to irritate
prostrate	lying down	**abyss**	bottomless depth
martyr	one who suffers	**vulgar**	common
traverse	to cross	**undulate**	to wave
vivid	bright	**pallor**	paleness

Nothing
is stronger
than custom.

- Ovid
43 B.C. - 18 A.D.

Caesar's English
Vocabulary from Latin
Lesson Eighteen

1. **apprehension**: fear
2. **superfluous**: extra
3. **tangible**: touchable
4. **lurid**: sensational
5. **pervade**: spread throughout

apprehension

At first, when we notice that the English noun **apprehension** can mean both understanding and fear, we might sense a problem, because these definitions seem like two very different things. But when we look closely at the Latin elements that compose the word, we begin to understand. **Apprehension** contains *ap* (a form of *ad*) meaning toward, *pre*, meaning before, and *hend*, to grasp. In fact, the Latin word *apprehendere* meant to grasp. So how does **apprehension** mean understanding? Well, even in modern English, we say the same thing; we say that someone is able to *grasp* a concept—it's the same idea! And when **apprehension** means fear, there is also a modern English equivalent: we say that someone is *gripped* by fear. Both in understanding and in fear, there is a kind of grasping something that is in front of you. Many wonderful writers have used **apprehension**, or its adjective form **apprehensive**, or its adverb form **apprehensively**, in their writing. In Natalie Babbitt's *Tuck Everlasting, a* character is "stiff with apprehension." In Jack London's novel *The Call of the Wild*, the dog, Buck, "watched them apprehensively." Do you guess this sentence means that Buck understood or that Buck was afraid? In H.G. Wells's *The War of the Worlds*, about Mars invading the Earth, there are "a thousand cities, chilled by ghastly apprehensions." In Robert Louis Stevenson's classic pirate adventure, *Treasure Island*, we find "the worst of my apprehensions realised." And Mark Twain, in *Tom Sawyer,* wrote that "The slow days drifted on, and each left behind it a slightly lightened weight of apprehension."

superfluous

Our English adjective **superfluous** comes straight from the Roman Latin, where it was spelled *superfluus*. **Superfluous** means extra, more than needed, excessive, unnecessary. In Jack London's *Call of the Wild*, the attempt to lighten the load on a dogsled by throwing away unneeded items is described as "the inexorable elimination of the superfluous." The word *inexorable* in London's sentence means inevitable, inescapable. In the same book, a dog is in "splendid condition, without an ounce of superfluous flesh." In Sir Walter Scott's 1820 classic of knighthood, *Ivanhoe*, there is "superfluous wealth," something we all wish we had! In Alfred Lansing's great account of the doomed Shackleton expedition to Antarctica, *Endurance*, the leader Shackleton requires his men to get rid of everything that was not necessary to carry, and the "only superfluous item Shackleton permitted was Worsley's diary." In Ralph Ellison's *Invisible Man*, we learn not to "waste time with superfluous questions," although in the classroom questions are such a good thing that it is hard to think of any question as superfluous. In George Eliot's classic novel, *Silas Marner*, there are "rich and stout husbands, whose wives had superfluous stores of linen." One of the greatest **superfluous** sentences in American literature comes from Henry David Thoreau's 1854 masterpiece, *Walden*, where he delivers the dictum that "Superfluous wealth can buy superfluities only."

We remember **superfluous** as an Advanced Word from an earlier chapter; now we see the strong role it has played in great literature.

tangible

In ancient Rome, the Latin verb *tangere* meant to touch, and today we extend this word into new life with English words such as *tangent*, and **tangible**. The adjective **tangible** means touchable, and its opposite **intangible** refers to things that can not be touched. For example, the tangible benefit of a job would include a paycheck, but the intangible benefit of a job might include the freedom to set your own schedule or the pride you feel at having that job. Sometimes the word **tangible** is used very poetically, as when Marjorie Rawlings writes in *The Yearling* that "Darkness came tangibly into the house, adding its heaviness to theirs." Imagine, darkness that you could almost touch! In Frank and Ernestine Gilbreth's book *Cheaper by the Dozen*, they write that "we were only average or below in some intangibles such as leadership and sociability." Why is leadership an intangible? In Jack London's *Call of the Wild*, the great dog Buck hears the howl of wolves in the forest: "Sometimes he pursued the call into the forest, looking for it as though it were a tangible thing." Mark Twain wrote, in his 1876 novel, *Tom Sawyer*, that "She swung downward and clawed at the intangible air." And in 1726, Jonathan Swift wrote in *Gulliver's Travels* that "Some were condensing air into a dry tangible substance." That sounds like a good trick!

lurid

Our English adjective **lurid** is a modern echo of the ancient Latin *luridus*, which meant sallow or ghastly. Something that is **lurid** is horrible, gruesome, sensational. We also use **lurid** to describe something that glows unnaturally, or that is garishly red. There can be lurid sunsets, lurid crimes, and lurid stories. There might be lurid details in the description of a battle. One great **lurid** sentence comes from George Orwell, who wrote, in his 1949 novel *1984*, that "It was night, and the white faces and the scarlet banners were luridly floodlit." In Kenneth

Grahame's *The Wind in the Willows*, one of the animals has "such lurid and imaginative cheek"; *cheek* in this context means nerve, or gall. In Stephen Crane's *The Red Badge of Courage*, a soldier bawls "in a lurid rage," and there is another whose "eyes were fixed in a lurid glare." From what you now know about the word **lurid**, what do you think a lurid glare would look like? In H.G. Wells's great science fiction classic, *The War of the Worlds*, "The sun…seemed blood red, and threw an unfamiliar lurid light upon everything." Sometimes **lurid** is used in a metaphorical way, which means as a poetic comparison; for example, in Harriet Beecher Stowe's 1851 *Uncle Tom's Cabin*, we read that "A softness gathered over the lurid fires of her eyes." What do you think Stowe meant by that? One of the best **lurid** sentences comes from Joseph Conrad in *Lord Jim*; Conrad wrote that "Vanity plays lurid tricks with our memory." Do you agree with Conrad?

pervade

The English verb **pervade** comes from the Latin *pervadere*, to pass through. *Per* meant through, and *vadere* meant go or walk. We use **pervade** when something spreads throughout something, or permeates it. In James M. Barrie's great *Peter Pan*, we read that "a deathly silence pervaded the island." In *Silent Spring*, Rachel Carson warned us about "the infinite number of man-made substances that now pervade our world"; she especially meant poisons, such as herbicides and insecticides. Martin Luther King used **pervade** in *Why We Can't Wait*: "As we talked," he wrote, "a sense of doom began to pervade the room." In *Tom Sawyer* Mark Twain wrote of "the pervading silence" and of "the deep pervading calm and silence of the woods." Many writers have used **pervade** to describe silence; in *Wuthering Heights* Emily Brontë wrote of "an austere silence pervading while we discussed our meal." Notice that **austere** is another word that we will learn in this chapter. A great **pervade** sentence comes from

Washington Irving's story *The Legend of Sleepy Hollow*; Irving wrote that "A drowsy, dreamy influence seems to hang over the land, and to pervade the very atmosphere." Of course, some of us think a drowsy, dreamy influence pervades our entire lives!

Real Latin
From Pliny the Younger:

Nullus est liber tam malus ut non aliqua parte posit.

There is no book so bad that it is not profitable in some part.

Who's That Author?
George Eliot, the author of *Silas Marner*, was born in 1819 as Mary Ann Evans in Chilvers Coton, Warwickshire. She attended a local school and then a boarding school in Coventry. She became self-taught after the age of seventeen, when she returned home to care for her ailing father. She became the editor of the *Westminster Review*, and knew the leading literary figures of her day. She began writing fiction in 1856 under the male pseudonym *George Eliot*, and concealed her real identity for years. Her greatest works are *Adam Bede*, *The Mill on the Floss*, *Silas Marner*, and *Middlemarch*. In her own time, she was admired by the American poet Emily Dickinson, and in modern times she has been influential on many writers, including Virginia Woolf. She died in London in 1880.

What is This Writer Saying?

Discuss the meaning of the **bold** word in each of the following sentences:

From Henry David Thoreau's *Walden*: "There is another alternative than to obtain the **superfluities**"

From Jack London's *The Call of the Wild*: "Buck watched them **apprehensively**."

From Marjorie Rawlings's *The Yearling*: "Darkness came **tangibly** into the house, adding its heaviness to theirs.

From Joseph Conrad's *Lord Jim*: "Vanity plays **lurid** tricks with our memory."

From Eudora Welty's *One Writer's Beginnings*: "The smell of being unvisited would **pervade, pervade, pervade**."

A Roman Fact

In 54 B.C., the Gallic leader Vercingetorix lead a rebellion against Julius Caesar. Preaching the unity of Gauls, Vercingetorix succeeded in a series of battles with Caesar, even defeating him at times. At length, Vercingetorix and his army were trapped on a hilltop, which Caesar surrounded and beseiged, even as he was being attacked by other Gallic armies trying to free Vercingetorix. In the end, Vercingetorix surrendered to Caesar, was taken back to Rome, displayed, and eventually executed. Today he is a national hero in France.

tangible

touchable

What now appeared
certain and tangible
happiness, might
soon dissipate into an airy dream.

-Mary Shelley
Frankenstein

Caesar's Synonyms

Here are words that are similar to the words in our list, but are they exactly the same in meaning? Or are they slightly different? For each word on our list, look up any synonym that you do not know, then pick one, and carefully explain the difference between it and our word.

apprehension: anxiety, uneasiness, worry, angst, misgiving, foreboding

superfluous: extra, excess, overflow, over the limit, redundant

tangible: touchable, concrete, material, palpable, physical, corporeal

lurid: gruesome, gaudy, flamboyant, flashy, ostentatious, meretricious

pervade: permeate, saturate, suffuse, flood, imbue, soak,

Julius Caesar, from his *Commentaries on the Gallic Wars*:

Though the Gauls are hasty and impetuous in going to war, they do not have the toughness and character necessary to stand up against Roman reserves.

Caesar's Spanish

Everywhere we turn, language reveals to us that modern English and modern Spanish are both descendants of ancient Latin:

Latin	Spanish	English
apprehendere	aprehensión	apprehension
superfluus	superfluo	superfluous
tangere	tangible	tangible

A Wordy Story...

A subtle feeling of apprehension began to pervade the placid villages, as vulgar, lurid reports of the Roman invasion filtered in. Surely, the odious might of the Roman empire would not be again visited upon the Gauls, who desired nothing more than a sanguine, serene, and amiable repose...But no, the reports kept coming, like water through the aqueducts, vivid reports of malevolent attacks, and of martyrdoms. Signs were manifest that the Romans were coming.

With pallid, melancholy visages and wistful memories, the Gauls began to brace for the prodigious onslaught, and the grotesque events that were soon to descend upon them. Even now, the Roman legions were traversing the gently undulating plain in the adjacent valley, and an abyss of dejection opened in the attitudes of the populace, who had been vexed enough when the spring crop failed in the drought.

One venerable chieftain, Vercingetorix, had clamored for unity among the tribes. Only by joining forces, he remonstrated with sagacity, could the Gauls hope to resist the power of Caesar's legions. "We must not," he cried, "fall prostrate before the condescending countenance of the conqueror, but we must force the vexing Roman evil to abate." Vercingetorix's singular confidence perplexed the incredulous and tremulous tribesmen, but slowly, a sublime dream dawned, an exquisite hope, that one day the profound words of this articulate leader could come true, and the specious omnipotence of Roman power would be exposed.

Caesar's Rewrites

Here are some sentences from famous books. In each case, rewrite the sentence into more ordinary words. Example from Marjorie Rawlings's *The Yearling*: "A languor crept over him." The rewrite: Little by little, he began to feel lazy.

From Jonathan Swift's *Gulliver's Travels*: "Some were condensing air into a dry **tangible** substance."

From Mark Twain's *Tom Sawyer*: "The slow days drifted on, and each left behind it a slightly lightened weight of **apprehension**."

From Henry David Thoreau's *Walden*: "**Superfluous** wealth can buy superfluities only."

From Stephen Crane's *The Red Badge of Courage*: "His eyes were fixed in a **lurid** glare."

From James M. Barrie's *Peter Pan*: "A deathly silence **pervaded** the island."

Caesar's Favorite Word

Think carefully about each of the words in this lesson, and predict which of these Caesar's English words you think you will use most often. Explain why you made this word your choice, and give at least three examples of situations in which you could use that word.

Caesar's Antonyms

For each of Caesar's English words in this lesson, think of a word that means the opposite.

 1. **apprehension**
 2. **superfluous**
 3. **tangible**
 4. **lurid**
 5. **pervade**

Are there any words in this list that have no antonyms? Are there any that it is very difficult to think of an antonym for? Why?

Caesar's Analogies

Analogies are about relationships. Find a second pair of words that have the same relationship to each other as the first pair has. Remember that it sometimes helps to put the two words into a sentence that makes the relationship clear.

TANGIBLE : PALPABLE ::
 a. austere : ascetic
 b. superfluous : insufficient
 c. stolid : visage
 d. genial : aloof

APPREHENSION : EMOTION ::
 a. superfluous : verbose
 b. martyr : hero
 c. stolid : unemotional
 d. palpable : tangible

Review for Cumulative Quiz

bi	two	**sub**	under
de	down	**pre**	before
super	over	**un**	not
inter	between	**semi**	half
dis	away	**sym**	together
circum	around	**mal**	bad
post	after	**equi**	equal
ante	before	**aqua**	water
audi	hear	**scrib**	write
cede	go	**cise**	cut
cred	believe	**miss**	send
cide	kill	**dict**	say
bell	war	**spec**	look
pend	hang	**omni**	all
re	again	**ex**	out
bene	good	**son**	sound
nov	new	**sangui**	blood
cogn	know	**ject**	throw
dorm	sleep	**magn**	great
ver	true	**put**	think
archy	government	**bio**	life
auto	self	**chron**	time
dec	ten		

countenance	facial expression	**profound**	deep
manifest	obvious	**prodigious**	huge
languor	weakness	**serene**	calm
acute	sharp	**grotesque**	distorted
condescend	to patronize	**odious**	hateful
exquisite	beautifully made	**clamor**	outcry
sublime	lofty	**tremulous**	quivering
allude	indirectly refer to	**placid**	calm
singular	unique	**amiable**	friendly
incredulous	skeptical	**perplex**	confuse
melancholy	sadness	**visage**	the face
venerate	to respect	**abate**	to lessen
repose	resting	**wistful**	yearning
subtle	slight	**sagacity**	wisdom
remonstrate	to object	**tedious**	boring
articulate	express clearly	**vex**	to irritate
prostrate	lying down	**abyss**	bottomless depth
martyr	one who suffers	**apprehension**	fear
superfluous	extra	**tangible**	touchable
lurid	sensational	**pervade**	spread throughout
vulgar	common	**traverse**	to cross
undulate	to wave	**vivid**	bright
pallor	paleness		

superfluous
extra

Superfluous wealth
can buy
superfluities only.

-Henry David Thoreau
Walden

Caesar's English
Ancient Latin Stems
Lesson Nineteen

Latin Stem List

stem	meaning	examples
geo*	(earth)	geography, geology, geometry
scope*	(look)	telescope, microscope, periscope
anti*	(against)	anti-aircraft, anticlimax, antithesis
intro	(into)	introduce, introspective, introvert
neo*	(new)	neon, neolithic, neophyte

* Of Greek Origin

Latin Stem Talk

GEO means earth. *Geography* is the study of the Earth's features; *geology* is the study of the Earth's rocks and rock structures, and *geometry* is a kind of mathematics that began with the effort to measure spaces on the Earth!

SCOPE means look. A *telescope* lets us look far, a *microscope* lets us look at small things, and a *periscope* lets us look around corners!

ANTI means against. An *anti-aircraft* gun is used against invading aircraft, an *anticlimax* is something in a story that spoils the conclusion, and an *antithesis* is an idea that is the opposite of another one!

INTRO means into. To *introduce* is to provide information that leads someone into something, *introspective* means looking into yourself thoughtfully, and an *introvert* is a person who is usually introspective, who is turned into himself!

NEO means new. *Neon* was a new gas that was discovered, the *neolithic* age was the New Stone Age, and a *neophyte* is a beginner!

Caesar's Analogy

The first two words are related to each other in a special way. Is one before the other? Is one inside the other? Are they opposites? Find the pair below that has the same relationship as the first pair!

NEOPHYTE : VETERAN ::
    a. telescope : microscope
    b. geography : earth
    c. introduction : book
    d. geometry : mathematics

Advanced Word: Neophyte

The English noun **neophyte**, from the Latin *neophytus*, which came from the Greek *neophytos*, means a beginner, but this word really comes to us from the science of biology, where a neophyte is a new (neo) plant (phyte); it the little baby plant that just pokes through the ground and spreads its two little leaves! In Charlotte Brontë's great 1847 novel, *Jane Eyre*, we read, "You have no right to preach to me, you neophyte."

Advanced Word: Introspective

In the adjective **introspective**, the modifying form of the noun **introspection**, we see an image of someone looking (spect) into (intro) themselves. Since we can't really see into ourselves, **introspection** really means thinking deeply about your own personal feelings and thoughts. In his 1850 novel *The Scarlet Letter*, Nathaniel Hawthorne described "an introspection so profound and acute." On the other hand, in *The American* Henry James described someone less thoughtful, with "the expression of his clear bright eye, completely void of introspection." In his 1903 *The Call of the Wild*, Jack London wrote that "Joe was the very opposite, sour and introspective," and Joseph Heller described the "massive, dull stare of moody introspection." And in H.G. Wells's classic *The Time Machine*, "He lapsed into an introspective state."

Which of these examples of **introspective** do you like best?

How many different meanings of **introspective** do you see?

How many of these novels that use **introspective** have you heard of before?

Who's That Writer?

In 1903 Jack London published his masterpiece, *The Call of the Wild*, about a dog, Buck, who becomes wild, rejects his tame qualities, and joins the wolves in Alaska. London's clear, tough writing made him very popular, and his theme of the wild potential within us all made readers think. London was born John Griffith London in San Francisco in 1876, and led an adventurous life doing odd jobs, joining the Alaska gold rush, and going to sea. In addition to *The Call of the Wild, his* novels *White Fang* and *The Sea Wolf* are still very popular today. London wrote more than fifty books and died in 1916.

Caesar's Spanish

stem	meaning	English / Spanish examples
geo	(earth)	geography / geografía
scope	(look)	telescope / telescopio
anti	(against)	anti-aircraft / antiaéreo
intro	(into)	introspective / introspectivo
neo	(new)	neophyte / neófito

Once again, we see the close alignment of English and Spanish vocabulary, illustrating how both languages come from the same ancient tongue.

A Roman Fact

Julius Caesar created the first newspaper, by having clerks record the proceedings in the Roman Senate and posting these *Acta Diurna* (Daily Deeds), on the walls of the forums. The news was then copied and distributed throughout the empire.

Real Latin

Galli pollicentur se facturos, quae.

The Gauls promise they will do what Caesar shall order.

Caesar's Word Search

In the box below, find the Latin-based English words. They might be vertical, horizontal, or at angles. Circle each word that you find

```
A N T I A I R C R A F T S I
P I M L T E L E S C O P E N
M N C G G F U S C V P N A T
I T J E E N B R F G U E N R
C R M M O R M B Z E P O T O
R O Q E L C H Q Y O N L I S
O V N H O K Y R C G E I C P
S E F H G S T S T R O T L E
C R M G Y E I L T A P H I C
O T V T M R L P U P H I M T
P U Y O E V E X Q H Y C A I
E F E P E L G N S Y T R X V
S G I N T R O D U C E C O E
A N T I T H E S I S K E E E
```

__ GEOGRAPHY   __ GEOLOGY   __ GEOMETRY   __ TELESCOPE

__ MICROSCOPE   __ PERISCOPE   __ ANTIAIRCRAFT   __ ANTICLIMAX

__ ANTITHESIS   __ INTRODUCE   __ INTROSPECTIVE   __ INTROVERT

__ NEON   __ NEOLITHIC   __ NEOPHYTE

Julius Caesar, from his *Commentaries on the Gallic Wars*:

The Belgae attack a fort just like the other Gauls do. They surround the whole wall with masses of men and shower rocks from all sides, forcing the defenders off. Then they move in with their shields over their heads and assail the wall.

Review for Cumulative Quiz

bi	two	**sub**	under
de	down	**pre**	before
super	over	**un**	not
inter	between	**semi**	half
dis	away	**sym**	together
circum	around	**mal**	bad
post	after	**equi**	equal
ante	before	**aqua**	water
audi	hear	**scrib**	write
cede	go	**cise**	cut
cred	believe	**miss**	send
cide	kill	**dict**	say
bell	war	**spec**	look
pend	hang	**omni**	all
re	again	**ex**	out
bene	good	**son**	sound
nov	new	**sangui**	blood
cogn	know	**ject**	throw
dorm	sleep	**magn**	great
ver	true	**put**	think
archy	government	**bio**	life
auto	self	**chron**	time
dec	ten	**geo**	earth
scope	look	**anti**	against
intro	into	**neo**	new

countenance	facial expression	**profound**	deep
manifest	obvious	**prodigious**	huge
languor	weakness	**serene**	calm
acute	sharp	**grotesque**	distorted
condescend	to patronize	**odious**	hateful
exquisite	beautifully made	**clamor**	outcry
sublime	lofty	**tremulous**	quivering
allude	indirectly refer to	**placid**	calm
singular	unique	**amiable**	friendly
incredulous	skeptical	**perplex**	confuse
melancholy	sadness	**visage**	the face
venerate	to respect	**abate**	to lessen
repose	resting	**wistful**	yearning
subtle	slight	**sagacity**	wisdom
remonstrate	to object	**tedious**	boring
articulate	express clearly	**vex**	to irritate
prostrate	lying down	**abyss**	bottomless depth
martyr	one who suffers	**apprehension**	fear
superfluous	extra	**tangible**	touchable
lurid	sensational	**pervade**	spread throughout
vulgar	common	**traverse**	to cross
undulate	to wave	**vivid**	bright
pallor	paleness		

I do not distinguish
by the eye,
but by the mind,
which is
the proper judge
of the man.

- Seneca
8 B.C. - 65 A.D.

Caesar's English
Vocabulary from Latin
Lesson Twenty

1. **genial**: kind
2. **stolid**: unemotional
3. **palpable**: touchable
4. **austere**: bare
5. **furtive**: stealthy

genial

In ancient Rome, *genialis* referred to someone who was festive, jovial, pleasant. Today, we still describe someone who is kind or warm to us as **genial**. Without knowing it, it seems, we speak Latin half the time! In *Peter Pan*, James M. Barrie describes Pirate Smee as "an oddly genial man." In Mark Twain's *Tom Sawyer*, there is "the magical thrill imparted by her genial touch," not to mention a character who is "mellow almost to the verge of geniality." In Bram Stoker's *Dracula*, there is "a little crowd of bicyclists and others who were genially noisy." Robert Louis Stevenson wrote, in *Kidnapped*, that "It was all uttered with a fine geniality of eye and manner which went far to conquer my distrust." What do you think Stevenson meant by a "fine geniality of eye"? Sometimes **genial** is used in a personification, which is describing an object as though it were human, with feelings; for example, in *Wuthering Heights* Emily Brontë wrote of "the salubrious air and genial sun." Her word *salubrious* means healthful. What would the genial sun be like? A great **genial** sentence comes from Herman Melville's immortal classic of the sea and the soul, *Moby Dick*, in which Captain Ahab devotes his life to the search for the great white whale. Melville wrote that "There is nothing like the perils of whaling to breed this free and easy sort of genial, desperado philosophy." In Mary Shelley's novel *Frankenstein*, she wrote that "The pleasant showers and genial warmth of spring greatly altered the aspect of the earth"; again, we see **genial** used in a personification.

stolid

Stolid means unemotional, impassive. When someone stands, flat-faced and unmoved, with little response, we call him or her **stolid**. This adjective comes from the Latin *stolidus*, which meant immovable, or even stupid, over 2,000 years ago in Rome. It is an interesting idea, that there would be a connection between being unmoved and being stupid! Perhaps the idea is that the brighter you are, the more you see, and the more you care. In Marjorie Kinnan Rawlings's 1938 American classic, *The Yearling*, we learn that "Ma Baxter received the news stolidly," and that "She dropped back to the ground and walked stolidly back into the house." What do you think it means, to walk stolidly? In Stephen Crane's great war novel, *The Red Badge of Courage*, we find the adjective **stolid** used to modify the noun *guns*: "The guns, stolid and undaunted, spoke with dogged valor." Why would Crane describe cannon as stolid? In Pearl Buck's novel, *The Good Earth*, we read that "They had worked and been silent, enduring stolidly the snow and ice under their bare, straw-sandalled feet." Mark Twain used **stolid** in *Tom Sawyer*: "And the poor creature dropped on his knees before the stolid murderer, and clasped his appealing hands." Twain also described "the stolid face of Injun Joe."

palpable

Our English adjective **palpable** means touchable, tangible, easily seen. It is a synonym of *obvious* and of *manifest*. We inherit this word from the Roman *palpabilis*, which meant touchable. One of the great **palpable** sentences comes from Martin Luther King, who wrote in

Why We Can't Wait, "When the cry for justice has hardened into a palpable force, it becomes irresistible." In *Tom Sawyer*, Mark Twain wrote, "Company would be a palpable improvement, he thought." In describing what a life at sea gives to a mariner, Herman Melville wrote in *Moby Dick* that most landsmen are ignorant "of some of the plainest and most palpable wonders of the world." In *1984* George Orwell wrote that "the most palpable facts can be denied or disregarded." He is surely right, unfortunately. Harriet Beecher Stowe, in *Uncle Tom's Cabin*, described "dire misrule, and palpable, unrebuked injustice." To rebuke is to criticize severely; *rebuke* is also a classic word that is used by many great writers, but it is Germanic in origin, rather than Latin. What do you think Stowe meant by palpable injustice? In the sword fight at the end of *Hamlet*, Shakespeare's 1601 masterpiece, there is a "hit, a very palpable hit."

It is interesting that we sometimes use **palpable** to describe things that can *not* be touched or seen, but we use it anyway to make the point, to express what a strong impression something has made on us. In *I Know Why the Caged Bird Sings*, Maya Angelou wrote that "The ugliness they left was palpable."

austere

The English adjective **austere** comes from the Latin *austerus*, which in turn came from the ancient Greek *austeros*, which meant harsh, rough, or bitter. It still means the same thing: bare, severe, stern, ascetic. When people are very solemn, they are austere. If someone is so self-disciplined that he lives a Spartan life without any luxuries or comforts, then he is austere. An austere room is stripped down, bare, unornamented. In *The Double Helix*, James Watson described research scientist Rosalind Franklin: "Her dedicated, austere life could not be thus explained." In John Knowles's *A Separate Peace*, there is "an untouched grove of pine, austere and beautiful." What do you think Robert Louis Stevenson meant in *Dr. Jekyll and Mr. Hyde* when he wrote that "He was austere with himself"? In *The Secret Garden*, Frances Hodgson Burnett wrote, "'I told you he was a charmer,' said Colin austerely." What does it mean, to speak austerely? In Jonathan Swift's 1726 masterpiece, *Gulliver's Travels*, we discover "a prince of much gravity, and austere countenance." What would the opposite of an austere countenance be? Do you remember seeing **austere** when we looked at **pervade**? In *Wuthering Heights* Emily Brontë wrote of "an austere silence pervading while we discussed our meal."

furtive

The adjective **furtive** has a wonderful origin. We use it to mean stealthy, sneaky, or surreptitious, but it traces back through the Latin *furtivus* to the noun *furtus*, theft. And so when something is furtive, it is done like a thief! In Nobel Prize winner William Golding's 1954 novel *The Lord of the Flies*, a boy "became less a hunter than a furtive thing, ape-like among the tangle of trees." Sneaky—in Ralph Ellison's *Invisible Man*, we read that "when I took a furtive glance around no one was paying me the slightest attention." In Marjorie Kinnan Rawlings's *The Yearling*, "The boy watched him furtively, then came behind him without speaking and picked up bits, too, and hurled them at the tree." H.G. Wells, in *The War of the Worlds*, wrote that the landscape was "quite silent and deserted, save for a few furtive plunderers hunting for food." In *Tom Sawyer*, Mark Twain wrote that "Presently the boy began to steal furtive glances at the girl."

Furtive glances—this adjective/noun pair has a distinguished history. We find furtive glances in Ellison's *Invisible Man*, in Thornton Wilder's *The Bridge of San Luis Rey*, in Virginia Wolfe's *Mrs. Dalloway*, in Kipling's *Kim*, in Twain's *Tom Sawyer*, in Stowe's *Uncle Tom's Cabin*, and in James Fennimore Cooper's *The Last of the Mohicans*. What do you think a furtive glance looks like?

Who's That Writer?

Frances Hodgson Burnett, the author of *The Secret Garden*, was born in 1849 in Manchester, England. In 1865 her family moved to the United States and settled in Knoxville, Tennessee. By 1868 she was a published writer, and began a long series of magazine articles and novels, leading to *Little Lord Fauntleroy* in 1886 and *The Secret Garden* in 1909. It has been said that the appearance of *Little Lord Fauntleroy* was based on the image of Oscar Wilde as a boy. Burnette wrote more than forty novels. At the end of her life she lived alternately in England and New York, where she died in 1924.

Real Latin

Modeste viras.
Live temperately.

What Is This Writer Saying?

Discuss the meaning of the **bold** word in each of the following sentences:

From Mark Twain's *Tom Sawyer*: "Company would be a **palpable** improvement, he thought."

From Thomas Hardy's *The Mayor of Casterbridge*: "Henchard's face settled into an expression of **stolid** loneliness which gradually modulated into something softer."

From Henry James's *The American*: "Valentin made a **genial** grimace."

From Mark Twain's *Tom Sawyer*: "Presently the boy began to steal **furtive** glances at the girl."

From Robert Louis Stevenson's Dr. Jekyll and Mr. Hyde: "He was **austere** with himself."

austere

bare, ascetic

An austere silence
pervaded while
we discussed our meal.

-Emily Brontë
Wuthering Heights

192

192

Caesar's Spanish

Everywhere we turn, language reveals to us that modern English and modern Spanish are both descendants of ancient Latin:

Latin	Spanish	English
genialis	genial	genial
stolidus	estólido	stolid
palpabilis	palpable	palpable
austerus	austero	austere
furtivus	furtivo	furtive

Caesar's Synonyms

Here are words that are similar to the words in our list, but are they exactly the same in meaning? Or are they slightly different? For each word on our list, look up any synonym that you do not know, then pick one, and carefully explain the difference between it and our word.

genial: friendly, amiable, good-natured, cordial, convivial, amicable

stolid: indifferent, apathetic, impassive, passive, passionless, inexpressive

palpable: concrete; sensible; detectable, observable, visible, tactile, evident

austere: bleak, bare, strict, unadorned, stark, grim, drab, severe, plain, barren

furtive: foxy, sharp, sneaky, stealthy, disingenuous, sly, oily, cunning, deceptive

A Wordy Story...

The captain was vexed beyond words, and it was manifest on his countenance. Although everything superfluous had been eliminated from the ship, the sublime abyss of space still loomed palpably ahead, and the instruments were tangible proof that the ship was slowing. The warning light emitted a lurid glow in the austere command tower, and the subordinates creeped furtively around, trying to avoid the captain's glaring visage, normally so genial and serene. Nearly prostrate with exhaustion, the crew worked on through the pervading apprehension, stolidly answering every command with compliance. A false, placid silence disguised the grotesque melancholy in the room; no one clamored for answers, and the captain was condescendingly amiable, but the profound danger of their situation perplexed all, and left a trace of singular incredulity on every face, but there was no remonstration. With each passing moment, the odious crisis became more acute. What sagacious tactic could increase the speed and get them to a safe port before the giant red star behind them, vivid and undulating with energy, exploded, making them traverse the great vacuum in a manner never envisioned by the astronautical engineers? If the situation did not abate soon, the pallor of apprehension would increase, all hope of repose would vanish, and a prodigious roar from behind would launch them forward at light speed, making them all martyrs to the future of space exploration. Only the captain, with his stolid self-confidence, seemed to believe that it would be okay, and that the exquisite abilities of humanity would prevail in the end. Incredulous and perplexed, all of the crew continued to watch him closely, and wait.

Caesar's Rewrites

Here are some sentences from famous books. In each case, rewrite the sentence into more ordinary words. Example from Marjorie Rawlings's *The Yearling*: "A languor crept over him." The rewrite: Little by little, he began to feel lazy.

From Mark Twain's *Tom Sawyer*: "Presently the boy began to steal **furtive** glances at the girl."

From Frances Hodgson Burnett's *The Secret Garden*: "'I told you he was a charmer,' said Colin **austerely**."

From Martin Luther King's *Why We Can't Wait*: "When the cry for justice has hardened into a **palpable** force, it becomes irresistible."

From Herman Melville's *Moby Dick*: "There is nothing like the perils of whaling to breed this free and easy sort of **genial**, desperado philosophy."

From Marjorie Rawlings's *The Yearling*: "Ma Baxter received the news **stolidly**."

Caesar's Favorite Word

Think carefully about each of the words in this lesson, and predict which of these Caesar's English words you think you will use most often. Explain why you made this word your choice, and give at least three examples of situations in which you could use that word.

Caesar's Antonyms

For each of Caesar's English words in this lesson, think of a word that means the opposite. A word that means the opposite is known as an **antonym**.

1. **genial**
2. **stolid**
3. **palpable**
4. **austere**
5. **furtive**

Are there any words in this list that have no antonyms? Are there any that it is very difficult to think of an antonym for? Why?

Caesar's Analogy

Analogies are about relationships. Find a second pair of words that have the same relationship to each other as the first pair has. Remember that it sometimes helps to put the two words into a sentence that makes the relationship clear.

THIEF : FURTIVE ::
a. stolid : effusive
b. palpable : manifest
c. odor : pervade
d. monastery : austere

Real Latin

Quid faciam.
What should I do?

Review for Cumulative Quiz

bi	two	**sub**	under
de	down	**pre**	before
super	over	**un**	not
inter	between	**semi**	half
dis	away	**sym**	together
circum	around	**mal**	bad
post	after	**equi**	equal
ante	before	**aqua**	water
audi	hear	**scrib**	write
cede	go	**cise**	cut
cred	believe	**miss**	send
cide	kill	**dict**	say
bell	war	**spec**	look
pend	hang	**omni**	all
re	again	**ex**	out
pallor	paleness	**bene**	good
son	sound	**nov**	new
sangui	blood	**cogn**	know
ject	throw	**dorm**	sleep
magn	great	**ver**	true
put	think	**archy**	government
bio	life	**auto**	self
chron	time	**dec**	ten
geo	earth	**scope**	look
anti	against	**intro**	into
neo	new		

Continued on next page...

countenance	facial expression	**profound**	deep
manifest	obvious	**prodigious**	huge
languor	weakness	**serene**	calm
acute	sharp	**grotesque**	distorted
condescend	to patronize	**odious**	hateful
exquisite	beautifully made	**clamor**	outcry
sublime	lofty	**tremulous**	quivering
allude	indirectly refer to	**placid**	calm
singular	unique	**amiable**	friendly
incredulous	skeptical	**perplex**	confuse
melancholy	sadness	**visage**	the face
venerate	to respect	**abate**	to lessen
vulgar	common	**traverse**	to cross
undulate	to wave	**vivid**	bright
repose	resting	**wistful**	yearning
subtle	slight	**sagacity**	wisdom
remonstrate	to object	**tedious**	boring
articulate	express clearly	**vex**	to irritate
prostrate	lying down	**abyss**	bottomless depth
martyr	one who suffers	**apprehension**	fear
superfluous	extra	**tangible**	touchable
lurid	sensational	**pervade**	spread throughout
genial	kind	**stolid**	unemotional
palpable	touchable	**austere**	bare
furtive	stealthy		

Caesar's English

The Latin Foundation of English Vocabulary for Elementary Scholars

Second Edition
Revised and Expanded

TEACHER'S MANUAL

Michael Clay Thompson
and
Myriam Borges Thompson

Royal Fireworks Press
Unionville, New York

Other Works By
Michael Clay Thompson

The Word Within The Word

The Magic Lens

Thinkers

Classic Words

Classics In The Classroom

Table of Contents

Introduction
INTRO - INTO
DUCT - LEAD

Caesar's English is offered as a preparatory complement to the *Word Within the Word* vocabulary program, volumes 1-3. Of course, this elementary program works just fine as a stand-alone vocabulary program for elementary students, but it also sets the stage for the more advanced program that should come in middle or high school.

The goals of *Caesar's English* are few, and strong. First, the program will illuminate, in students' minds, the age of their language, revealing its Roman beginnings. Second, the program teaches students fifty of the greatest Latin stems in English, showing their continuing presence in a host of modern English words. These stems are among the most common and valuable, and will provide an intellectual key for young students to understand that big words aren't necessarily hard. Third, therefore, the program deliberately discards the specious confines of age-graded vocabulary, on the sound observation that even little children can give the species names of the dinosaurs—a clear proof that they can learn and understand better words than they are usually asked to learn. Fourth, the program aims to sow the seeds of intellectuality by introducing students to the drama and romance of ancient Rome, to the names of its thinkers, and to some of the fascinating facts of its history. Fifth, the program shows the Latin-English-Spanish connection, indicating clearly how the two great languages of the United States are members of the same family and have the same old man.

Finally, in selecting example words that illustrate the use of these fifty Latin stems, we have chosen the best sentences we could find, even if a sentence was from a book students are more likely to read in high school than in elementary school. Although we deliberately included children's authors such as Sir Walter Scott, Frances Hodgson Burnett, Kenneth Grahame, and Robert Louis Stevenson, we also drew freely from famous authors generally, such as the Brontës and Jane Austen. The obvious advantage of this is that the students will see a great sentence, but a secondary advantage is that these bright elementary kids will begin to encounter famous literary names, such as Defoe and Milton, Morrison and Shelley, and subtly develop a sense of anticipation about reading these famous authors in the future.

It is our hope that teachers and students, far far away, will enjoy this book.

Michael Thompson and Myriam Borges Thompson
May, 2000

We little knew when we first released this book, how eager colleagues were for it, and how they would ask for more. Accordingly, and more quickly than is often the case with a revision, here is more. This revised edition of *Caesar's English* more than doubles the size of the first edition, complements the Latin stems with great, Latin-based, classic words from American and British literature, and increases the presence of Roman history that provides the intellectual foundation of the endeavor. Again, we hope very much that you enjoy this book.

Michael and Myriam Borges Thompson
December, 2000

Lesson Components

How to Use
the Features of
Caesar's English

Ancient Latin Stems

Every odd-numbered lesson begins with a list of five Latin stems, with brief definitions and three example words for each stem. These stems have been selected because they are Latin and because they are among the central, most important stems in English. The example words contain at least one word that is above grade level. Below the list of stems is a section, Latin Stem Talk, that introduces each stem to the students.

READ ALOUD: This section of stems and stem talk is best read aloud, slowly, with feeling, and one item at a time. Much of the content of this text is very advanced for elementary students—that is exactly the intent, to offer the most advanced vocabulary text ever assigned to elementary students—and it is therefore very important that the students' first encounter with the words, author's names, Roman terms, and so forth, be correct. We don't want to let the students develop initial habits of mispronunciation. Careful reading aloud, with different students taking different paragraphs, and pauses between paragraphs for short comments and discussions, is optimal.

Caesar's Analogies

There is no reason why young students can not begin to do analogies. It is good for them to understand the fundamental idea that analogies force you to focus on the invisible connection between two words, rather than on the words themselves. In order to see the invisible middle, you have to understand each term clearly.

Each lesson contains one or two analogies. These are best assigned either as homework or as small group problems, followed in either case by classroom review in which students present their reasoning. Keep in mind that very bright children often see relationships

1

unnoticed by others, and highly intelligent answers may emerge that are not in agreement with the answer given in this book. In such a case, review the reasons for the book answer while still praising the insight of the student answer.

Advanced Word: Superfluous

The Advanced Word segments of the stem lessons give students a chance to see a really advanced word, one that would never normally be studied by younger students in American schools. Again, these should be carefully read aloud and discussed. One good idea for the Advanced Words is to let them know that you will use them as extra point questions on the cumulative quizzes. You might just write on the blackboard, "What is the advanced word that means..." and let students supply the word you have defined.

Who's That Writer?

The word discussions in Caesar's English make routine reference to dozens of great writers from American and British literature. Many of these, such as Robert Louis Stevenson, Frances Hodgson Burnett, and Kenneth Grahame, are authors of children's books that elementary students can read immediately. Other authors, such as Ernest Hemingway, Jane Austen, and Scott Fitzgerald, are typically read in middle or high school, or even college. Even though the students will not be reading some of these books that are referred to, it will do no harm for them to begin hearing these famous names. The purpose of Who's That Writer? is to provide some background information so that students have at least an introductory education about the author's significance. It is highly recommended that the teacher read through this section with the students and share enthusiasm, telling the students a little bit more sometimes, and giving small reports to the students about his or her own favorite works by these authors the students have not yet read. There may very well be students in the class who are really ready for Tom Sawyer or another such book, and the teacher might like to offer credit for that work. It is also possible that a teacher would select a few of the titles from these discussions for reading by the class—this would allow the vocabulary program and reading program to reinforce each other.

Caesar's Spanish

Everyone who has acquired a close acquaintance with English, Spanish, and Latin knows that the two great languages of the contemporary United States are very close siblings, both descended primarily from the same ancient Latin, and sharing a vast overlap of common Latin stems and wonderfully similar cognates. The cognates presented in the Caesar's Spanish component are offered for view, as dazzling examples. They can be either read silently or aloud. It would be wonderful if bilingual teachers and/or students would piggyback on these examples to come up with more. Clearly, one purpose of this component is to increase respect for Spanish as a Romance language that shares its great intellectual heritage of Latin with English.

A Roman Fact

Throughout *Caesar's English*, there are fragments of Roman history, culture, and civilization. Sometimes these are simple facts that are fascinating and that are designed to lure the students in, inviting further research. The Roman Fact, the Real Latin, the quote from Julius Caesar's *Commentaries on the Gallic Wars*, the Discussion Poster, the graphic images, all of these are designed to associate inextricably English vocabulary and ancient Roman history, and to increase the intellectual content and fascination of the study.

Real Latin

The Real Latin quote in each lesson is a specimen, an ancient shard of the mind, that students can just look at. Its purpose is to perplex them and fascinate them, perhaps causing some of them to study Latin when they have a chance. In many cases, students will be able to work out what word means what, and they will have a more accurate feeling for Latin than if they had seen only the stems.

Julius Caesar, from his *Commentaries on the Gallic Wars*:

Many students today may not even realize that they can read a book written by Julius Caesar, and yet for generations school children were introduced to the life of the mind by translating Caesar's *Commentaries on the Gallic Wars* from Latin into English. The quotations here are another link to the historical language foundation, and have been selected to intrigue curious students, perhaps resulting in their doing further explorations on their own. One classroom idea is to follow up on these quotations or the ones in the posters with small research assignments, letting students show the class what else they found out.

Discussion Poster

The Discussion Poster is intended for Socratic discussion. The teacher should present the poster to the students, either on the wall or as a projection of a transparency, and conduct a discussion of the idea, letting the students explore the idea in an open-ended way. No right answer is provided, and none should be advocated by the teacher. Rather, all students should be encouraged to think, to piggyback on others' ideas, and to respect all other views. Some of the quotations are not so baffling that agreement will fail, but they will still allow for nuances and various qualities of description.

Caesar's Word Search

These, for some ineffable reason, are just fun. They are probably good for visual learners, and they give us a pain-free chance to internalize more great words that have

Latin foundations. The process of seeing them, pronouncing them, and finding them, will do no child harm.

Vocabulary from Latin

The odd-numbered chapters, be it recalled, are based on Latin stems. The even numbered chapters that alternate with them do not focus on stems, but on words that reach American English from the distant shores of ancient Rome. These Latin-based words (actually, there is one for fun that is not Latin but that offers an interesting comparison) have all been identified by Michael Thompson's *Classic Words* vocabulary research software (available as *Classic Words Pro* for teachers at www.classicwords.com) as among the most central literary words in the English language. For various of their merits, these particular Latin-based words have distinguished histories in English, and can be found in the preponderance of great works in American and British English. Students who study these words will enjoy a greater ease with reading, leading to a greater fluency in general. The alternation of Latin stem chapters with Latin-based vocabulary chapters gives *Caesar's English* a nice rhythm that students will enjoy.

The Vocabulary chapters begin with a short list of words with definitions, and then move to a series of short readings, one about each word in the list. These readings are intended to be read aloud. The teacher should read the first one, to model the style, which is slow and clear, pausing at the commas and periods, and emphasizing the life of the great quotes that are included in each reading. It is entirely appropriate to pause both during and after each reading to talk about the usages found, and to express enthusiasm for uses that are creative or brilliant. The more that each reading is encountered in this way, rather than just read quickly in a monotone, the more it will transfer into the student's thought. These readings are an especially good opportunity for intellectual leadership by the teacher, who can interject asides about famous authors or wonderful sentences, and liven the experience with personal contribution.

Note: Some of the quotations have a slash / like that in the middle of the line. This means that the quote was poetry, and the slash represents where the new line began in the poem.

What is This Writer Saying?

One of the most effective components in the lessons is the What Is This Writer Saying? component, which presents students with five sentences from famous authors, and asks them to explain the meaning of the sentence. Each sentence uses one of the words in the lesson. The point here is that author's use words with great fun and subtlety, and students will quickly find that the brief definition given at the beginning is minimal, and that to really explain the essence of the writer's intent, they will have to resort to other words, not provided for them.

Caesar's Synonyms

This section presents students with an array of words that are either synonyms, partial synonyms, or related words. The student should study each word and its relatives, look up any word not known, and then pick one of the related words to explain to the other students. The object is to make fine distinctions. We all know that rarely are synonyms truly exact. Subtle differences of emphasis, or style, or detail separate them. There are times when one would use countenance, or visage, or aspect, or face, or physiognomy, and a judicious selection of any over the others would be a mark of intellect. This activity lets students refine their subtle selection.

Caesar's Rewrites

Caesar's Rewrites is another activity that will strengthen memory and comprehension. We all know that if you can put something in your own words accurately, that is a sign of understanding. If students rewrite these five sentences, putting the idea into their own words—not just substituting the one lesson word with the lesson definition, but really rewriting the sentence—it will help to internalize the vocabulary. Then the follow is to read their revisions to the class and compare.

Caesar's Antonyms

The testing services may have discontinued antonyms from major tests, but that does not mean that thinking about antonyms is a bad idea. In fact, there are times when producing an antonym is decisive in understanding, as when we notice that *diffidence* is the opposite of *confidence*. This activity will let students try to produce antonyms for list words, generating some interesting thought and discussion in the process, as they realize that it is impossible to produce a true antonym for some words! This is another activity that can be done together. The teacher should let them work out antonyms either individually or in small groups, and then bring the whole class together to compare the answers for each one.

A Wordy Story

Each vocabulary lesson contains a Wordy Story, which combines all the big words that the students have learned into a single story. This should be read aloud in the class, two or three students taking turns, and then the teacher should go back through the story, sentence by sentence, having the students explain the meaning of each sentence. When this is done, one student should volunteer to retell the whole story in ordinary English. Part of the secret plan in the Wordy Story component is that if elementary students can read these stories, they can read *anything*.

Caesar's Favorite Word

The intent of this activity is to cause students to prefer. There is something involved in forming a preference that increases both understanding and appreciation. Students who do this in good faith and say that they like this word and think they will use it, are more likely to do so. This would be a good activity to assign for homework, asking the students to come in with a paragraph about the word they picked and why they picked it. Having several volunteer students read their choices before collecting papers would be a good influence on everyone.

Caesar's English Word Poster

Here is a nice poster to copy and put on the wall. They can build up over time. If you want to adopt a word-of-the-day or week approach, this would help.

Review for Cumulative Quiz

Each lesson concludes with a cumulative list of all stems and vocabulary words, so that students can easily review for the quiz. It is also a visual statement of the knowledge they are accumulating.

Cumulative Quiz

Each lesson contains a cumulative quiz that is found only in the teacher's manual. Students will have to study all stems and words, and will have to learn the words both from word to definition and from definition to word, in order to do well on the quiz.

Twenty Questions

The Twenty Questions component is intended for fun, not really for a grade. It is too difficult, probably, to count as a grade. Rather, it should be planned after every five lessons, in order to give the students a week off from learning a new list, and to give them rather a week in which they can thoughtfully review all the readings of the previous five lists in order to reread closely—as the Stoics recommended. Each teacher has ways of handling games like this, for it is, after all, a trivia game. The kids should know that it is coming, and a strategy such as dividing the class into two group that can compete to answer the most questions would give them some fun and excitement. I think it is better to reward the whole class for knowing so much than to reward the winning group only.

Caesar's English
Lesson One

Analogy

DESCEND : ASCEND ::
    a. bicycle : tricycle
    b. submerge : emerge
    c. man : superman
    d. school : preschool

Answer: b. **Submerge** and **emerge** are opposites, as **descend** and **ascend** are opposites.

Wordsearch

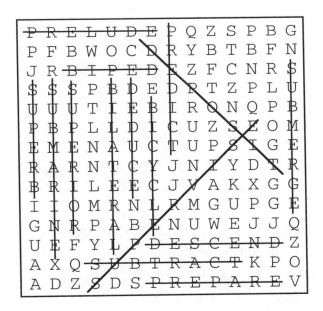

  __ BICYCLE   __ SUBMARINE   __ DESCEND   __ PREDICT
  __ SUPERVISE   __ BIPED   __ SUBMERGE   __ DEPOSIT
  __ PREPARE   __ SUPERIOR   __ BILATERAL   __ SUBTRACT
  __ DEDUCE   __ PRELUDE   __ SUPERB

Caesar's English
Lesson One Quiz

For each sentence, define the stem, not the word, that is in **bold**.

1. The artwork **de**picted a happy scene. _____
2. The nations made a **bi**lateral treaty. _____
3. She made a **super**cilious face. _____
4. The **sub**ordinate obeyed his officer. _____
5. Our plans were **pre**mature. _____

Caesar's English
Lesson One Quiz

1. The artwork **de**picted a happy scene. *down*
2. The nations made a **bi**lateral treaty. *two*
3. She made a **super**cilious face. *over*
4. The **sub**ordinate obeyed his officer. *under*
5. Our plans were **pre**mature. *before*

Caesar's English
Lesson Two

Analogies

MANIFEST : OBSERVABLE ::
a. acute : pain
b. odious : loveable
c. languor : weakness
d. condescend : admire

Answer: c. **Manifest** and **observable** are synonyms, as **languor** and **weakness** are synonyms.

WISDOM : PROFOUND ::
a. acute : blunt
b. prodigious : microscopic
c. countenance : expression
d. languor : weak

Answer: d. As **wisdom** can be **profound**, **languor** can be **weak**; the second term is a modifier of or a characteristic of the first.

9

Caesar's English
Cumulative Quiz • Lesson Two

A. Fill in the definition:
 1. languor _____
 2. profound_____
 3. countenance _____

B. Write in the Caesar's English Word:
 4. obvious_____
 5. huge _____

C. Define the stem in bold:
 6. **de**duce _____
 7. **super**b _____
 8. **bi**ped _____
 9. **pre**lude_____
 10. **sub**merge _____

Caesar's English
Cumulative Quiz • Lesson Two

A. Fill in the definition:
    1. languor *weakness*
    2. profound *deep*
    3. countenance *facial expression*

B. Write in the Caesar's English Word:
    4. obvious *manifest*
    5. huge *prodigious*

C. Define the stem in bold:
    6. **de**duce *down*
    7. **super**b *over*
    8. **bi**ped *two*
    9. **pre**lude *before*
    10. **sub**merge *under*

Caesar's English
Lesson Three

Analogy

INTERSTELLAR : STARS ::
   a. semicircle: circle
   b. dismiss: convene
   c. air : marbles
   d. unequal: equal

Answer: c. **Interstellar** space is between the **stars** as **air** is between the **marbles**.

Word Search

```
V H I S S D D Z K Z L T L E
M S Y S E S I O Y X A D U I
A Y I Y M M Y S E P B R N N
B M N M I U I M T N Q H D T
K P T M C N S F P R Y D O E
U A E I A Z A Q H A C N R R
D T R T R B R K T R O C E S
I H J R C L U E H T M N T T
S Y E Y L E I A Q M X A Y E
M X C T E X Y Q G E R N L L
I N T E R N A T I O N A L L
S J J M L U N E Q U A L O A
S U S I I D I S T O R T J R
S E M I A N N U A L Z J A K
```

__ UNEQUAL   __ INTERNATIONAL   __ SEMICIRCLE   __ DISMISS
__ SYMPHONY   __ UNABLE   __ INTERSTELLAR   __ SEMIFORMAL
__ DISTRACT   __ SYMPATHY   __ UNDONE   __ INTERJECT
__ SEMIANNUAL   __ DISTORT   __ SYMMETRY

12

Caesar's English
Cumulative Quiz • Lesson Three

For each sentence, define the stem, not the word, that is in **bold**.

1. His answer was **un**equivocal. _____
2. The design was **sym**metrical. _____
3. There was a brief **inter**lude. _____
4. The image was **dis**torted. _____
5. It was a **semi**aquatic species. _____
6. The glacier left a **de**posit of sediment. _____
7. Human beings are **bi**peds. _____
8. It was a **super**b book. _____
9. There was a **sub**terranean river. _____
10. The word *for* is a **pre**position. _____

For each sentence, define the word that is in **bold**.

11. His feelings were **manifest** on his face. _____
12. She had **profound** ideas. _____
13. The **languor** of the hot afternoon overcame Fido. _____
14. They beheld his angry **countenance**. _____
15. There was a **prodigious** uprorar. _____

13

Caesar's English
Cumulative Quiz • Lesson Three

For each sentence, define the stem, not the word, that is in **bold**.
1. His answer was **un**equivocal. *not*
2. The design was **sym**metrical. *together*
3. There was a brief **inter**lude *between*
4. The image was **dis**torted. *away*
5. It was a **semi**aquatic species. *half*
6. The glacier left a **de**posit of sediment. *down*
7. Human beings are **bi**peds. *two*
8. It was a **super**b book. *over*
9. There was a **sub**terranean river. *under*
10. The word *for* is a **pre**position. *before*

For each sentence, define the word that is in **bold.**
11. His feelings were **manifest** on his face. *obvious*
12. She had **profound** ideas. *deep*
13. The **languor** of the hot afternoon overcame Fido. *weakness*
14. They beheld his angry **countenance**. *facial expression*
15. There was a **prodigious** uprorar. *huge*

14

Analogy

SERENE: AGITATED::
   a. loud : quiet
   b. profound : deep
   c. odious : mask
   d. countenance : strange

Answer: a. **Serene** and **agitated** are opposites, as **loud** and **quiet** are opposites

Caesar's English
Cumulative Quiz • Lesson Four

For each sentence, define the word that is in **bold**.
1. An **odious** sneer crossed his face. _____
2. She felt an **acute** pain. _____
3. We woke to a **serene** sky. _____
4. His **condescending** air insulted us. _____
5. A **grotesque** shape loomed out of the shadow. _____
6. The reasons were **manifest**. _____
7. We looked into the **profound** abyss. _____
8. He felt a sense of increasing **languor**. _____
9. Her **countenance** was hidden from our eyes. _____
10. A **prodigious** blast came from the cannon. _____

For each sentence, define the stem, not the word, that is in **bold**.
11. We were **un**done. _____
12. She went to the **sym**phony. _____
13. It is an **inter**national law. _____
14. His mind was **dis**tracted. _____
15. We heard tones and **semi**tones. _____
16. They **de**cried the lack of equipment. _____
17. It takes a **bi**lateral agreement. _____
18. Avoid a **super**ior attitude. _____
19. What a **sub**lime thought. _____
20. She had a **pre**scient intuition. _____

16

Caesar's English
Lesson Four Quiz • Answer Key

For each sentence, define the word that is in **bold.**
1. An **odious** sneer crossed his face. *hateful*
2. She felt an **acute** pain. *sharp*
3. We woke to a **serene** sky. *calm*
4. His **condescending** air insulted us. *patronizing*
5. A **grotesque** shape loomed out of the shadow. *weird*
6. The reasons were **manifest**. *obvious*
7. We looked into the **profound** abyss. *deep*
8. He felt a sense of increasing **languor**. *weakness*
9. Her **countenance** was hidden from our eyes. *facial expression*
10. A **prodigious** blast came from the cannon. *huge*

For each sentence, define the stem, not the word, that is in **bold**.
11. We were **un**done. *not*
12. She went to the **sym**phony. *together*
13. It is an **inter**national law. *between*
14. His mind was **dis**tracted. *away*
15. We heard tones and **semi**tones. *half*
16. They **de**cried the lack of equipment. *down*
17. It takes a **bi**lateral agreement. *two*
18. Avoid a **super**ior attitude. *over*
19. What a **sub**lime thought. *under*
20. She had a **pre**scient intuition. *before*

17

Analogy

CIRCUMNAVIGATE: SHIP::
  a. postscript : letter
  b. antebellum: war
  c. orbit: satellite
  1d. equivocate: speaker

Answer: c. **Circumnavigate** is a ship going around the world, as an **orbit** is how a satellite goes around the world.

Word Search

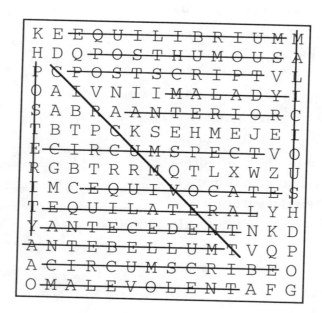

__ CIRCUMSCRIBE   __ CIRCUMSPECT   __ CIRCUMVENT   __ MALEVOLENT
__ MALADY   __ MALICIOUS   __ POSTHUMOUS   __ POSTSCRIPT
__ POSTERITY   __ EQUILATERAL   __ EQUIVOCATE   __ EQUILIBRIUM
__ ANTEBELLUM   __ ANTECEDENT   __ ANTERIOR

18

Caesar's English
Cumulative Quiz • Lesson Five

For each sentence, define the stem, not the word, that is in **bold**.

1. The ship **circum**navigated the globe. _____
2. The clown was not **mal**icious. _____
3. She added a **post**script to the letter. _____
4. It was an **equi**lateral triangle. _____
5. It was built in the **ante**bellum period. _____
6. They were **un**able to accept. _____
7. The **sym**phony was beautiful. _____
8. They blasted into **inter**stellar space. _____
9. The crowd was **dis**persed. _____
10. The dance was **semi**formal. _____
11. Sherlock **de**duced the truth. _____
12. The nations reached a **bi**lateral agreement. _____
13. Mom **super**vised the kids. _____
14. **Sub**tract three from four to get one. _____
15. The prophet **pre**dicted the future. _____

For each sentence, define the word that is in **bold**.

16. In the afternoon, a **languor** crept through his limbs. _____
17. The prophet was seized with a **profound** vision. _____
18. Signs of unrest were **manifest** in the crowd. _____
19. The witness had a curious **countenance**. _____
20. **Prodigious** flocks of birds descended. _____
21. The peak offered a **serene** vista. _____
22. **Odious** memories are not easily forgotten. _____
23. **Grotesque** faces stared from the painting. _____
24. One should not **condescend** to one's peers. _____
25. The two **acute** angles did not equal a right angle. _____

19

Caesar's English
Lesson Five Quiz • Answer Key

For each sentence, define the stem, not the word, that is in **bold**.

1. The ship **circum**navigated the globe.   *around*
2. The clown was not **mal**icious.   *bad*
3. She added a **post**script to the letter.   *after*
4. It was an **equi**lateral triangle.   *equal*
5. It was built in the **ante**bellum period.   *before*
6. They were **un**able to accept.   *not*
7. The **sym**phony was beautiful.   *together*
8. They blasted into **inter**stellar space.   *between*
9. The crowd was **dis**persed.   *away*
10. The dance was **semi**formal.   *half*
11. Sherlock **de**duced the truth.   *down*
12. The nations reached a **bi**lateral agreement.   *two*
13. Mom **super**vised the kids.   *over*
14. **Sub**tract three from four to get one.   *under*
15. The prophet **pre**dicted the future.   *before*

For each sentence, define the word that is in **bold**.

16. In the afternoon, a **languor** crept through his limbs.   *weakness*
17. The prophet was seized with a **profound** vision.   *deep*
18. Signs of unrest were **manifest** in the crowd.   *obvious*
19. The witness had a curious **countenance**.   *facial expression*
20. **Prodigious** flocks of birds descended.   *huge*
21. The peak offered a **serene** vista.   *calm*
22. **Odious** memories are not easily forgotten.   *hateful*
23. **Grotesque** faces stared from the painting.   *distorted*
24. One should not **condescend** to one's peers.   *to patronize*
25. The two **acute** angles did not equal a right angle.   *sharp*

20

Analogies

SUBLIME : PEDESTRIAN::
  a. amiable : peevish
  b. clamor : hubbub
  c. perplex : mystery
  d. clamor : riot

Answer: a. **Sublime** and **pedestrian** are opposites, as **amiable** and **peevish** are opposites

TREMULOUS : FEAR ::
  a. clamorous : anger
  b. incredulous : gullible
  c. sublime : noble
  d. amiable : person

Answer: a. Being **tremulous** is a sign of **fear**, as being **clamorous** is a sign of **anger**.

A. Fill in the definition.
1. exquisite _____
2. sublime _____
3. allude _____
4. manifest _____
5. prodigious _____
6. languor _____
7. allude _____
8. serene _____
9. grotesque _____
10. odious _____

B. Fill in the Caesar's English Word that is defined.
11. outcry _____
12. quivering _____
13. deep _____
14. facial expression _____
15. to patronize _____

C. Define the stem, not the word, that is in bold:
16. The **circum**ference was seven miles. _____
17. She was a famous **mal**content. _____
18. The document was **post**dated. _____
19. Garrison would not **equi**vocate. _____
20. Their **ante**room was larger than our house. _____
21. The solution was **un**acceptable. _____
22. The **sym**biotic species lived in harmony. _____
23. Chaos reigned during the **inter**regnum. _____
24. The **dis**tortions concealed the truth. _____
25. It was a **semi**annual event. _____

Caesar's English
Cumulative Quiz • Lesson Six

A. Fill in the definition.
1. exquisite *beautifully made*
2. sublime *lofty*
3. allude *indirectly refer to*
4. manifest *obvious*
5. prodigious *huge*
6. languor *weakness*
7. acute *sharp*
8. serene *calm*
9. grotesque *distorted*
10. odious *hateful*

B. Fill in the Caesar's English Word that is defined.
11. outcry *clamor*
12. quivering *tremulous*
13. deep *profound*
14. facial expression *countenance*
15. to patronize *condescend*

C. Define the stem, not the word, that is in bold:
16. The **circum**ference was seven miles. *around*
17. She was a famous **mal**content. *bad*
18. The document was **post**dated. *after*
19. Garrison would not **equi**vocate. *equal*
20. Their **ante**room was larger than our house. *before*
21. The solution was **un**acceptable. *not*
22. The **sym**biotic species lived in harmony. *together*
23. Chaos reigned during the **inter**regnum. *between*
24. The **dis**tortions concealed the truth. *away*
25. It was a **semi**annual event. *half*

23

Caesar's English
Lesson Seven

Analogy

SCRIBE : WRITES ::
   a. audience : hears
   b. audiophile : stereo
   c. incisive : speech
   d. aquarium : fish

Answer: a. A relationship of function: a scribe writes as an audience hears.

Word Search

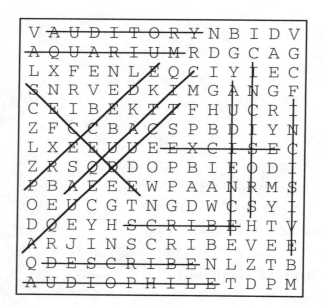

__ AQUATIC	__ AQUEDUCT	__ AQUARIUM	__ AUDITORY
__ AUDIENCE	__ AUDIOPHILE	__ SCRIBE	__ INSCRIBE
__ DESCRIBE	__ RECEDE	__ PRECEDE	__ SECEDE
__ EXCISE	__ INCISIVE	__ INCISORS	

Caesar's English
Cumulative Quiz • Lesson Seven

For each sentence, define the stem, not the word, that is in **bold**.

1. **Aqua**tic plants grew in the pond. _____
2. The injury damaged his **audi**tory nerve. _____
3. The pharaoh called loudly for his **scrib**e. _____
4. The incident set a poor pre**cede**nt. _____
5. Her in**cis**ive observations settled the dispute. _____
6. The **circum**stances were different this time. _____
7. A strange **mal**ady afflicted the settlement. _____
8. She wrote her memoirs for **post**erity to read. _____
9. The blow affected the **ante**rior portion of the brain. _____
10. We all felt **sym**pathy for the family. _____
11. Please send an **inter**departmental memo. _____
12. The fiesta was a **semi**annual event. _____
13. The crime was widely **de**nounced. _____
14. The stars form a **bi**nary system. _____
15. He continued with his **super**erogatory remarks. _____

For each sentence, define the word in bold.

16. A **sublime** hope filled the air. _____
17. The **tremulous** leaves made a peaceful sound. _____
18. Don't **allude** to the problem. _____
19. Her disappointment was **manifest**. _____
20. Her **acute** mind won the day. _____

For each definition, fill in the Caesar's English word.

21. deep _____
22. facial expression _____
23. distorted _____
24. outcry _____
25. beautifully made _____

Caesar's English
Cumulative Quiz • Lesson Seven

For each sentence, define the stem, not the word, that is in **bold**.
1. **Aqua**tic plants grew in the pond. *water*
2. The injury damaged his **audi**tory nerve. *hear*
3. The pharaoh called loudly for his **scrib**e. *write*
4. The incident set a poor pre**ced**ent. *go*
5. Her in**cis**ive observations settled the dispute. *cut*
6. The **circum**stances were different this time. *around*
7. A strange **mal**ady afflicted the settlement. *bad*
8. She wrote her memoirs for **post**erity to read. *after*
9. The blow affected the **ante**rior portion of the brain. *before*
10. We all felt **sym**pathy for the family. *together*
11. Please send an **inter**departmental memo. *between*
12. The fiesta was a **semi**annual event. *half*
13. The crime was widely **de**nounced. *down*
14. The stars form a **bi**nary system. *two*
15. He continued with his **super**erogatory remarks. *over*

For each sentence, define the word in **bold**.
16. A **sublime** hope filled the air. *lofty*
17. The **tremulous** leaves made a peaceful sound. *quivering*
18. Don't **allude** to the problem. *indirectly refer to*
19. Her disappointment was **manifest**. *obvious*
20. Her **acute** mind won the day. *sharp*

For each definition, fill in the Caesar's English word.
21. deep *profound*
22. facial expression *countenance*
23. distorted *grotesque*
24. outcry *clamor*
25. beautifully made *exquisite*

26

Analogy

   MIRACLE : INCREDULOUS ::
      a. placid : serene
      b. singular : common
      c. mystery : perplexed
      d. allude : refer

Answer: c. A matter of result—A **miracle** leaves people **incredulous**, as a **mystery** leaves people **perplexed**.

Caesar's English
Cumulative Quiz • Lesson Eight

A. Fill in the definition.
1. placid _____
2. grotesque _____
3. sublime _____
4. manifest _____
5. clamor _____
6. odious _____
7. allude _____
8. acute _____
9. perplex _____
10. prodigious _____

B. Write in the Caesar's English word for each definition.
11. friendly _____
12. facial expression _____
13. beautifully made _____
14. deep _____
15. quivering _____

C. Define the stem that is in **bold**.
16. They began to **scrib**ble furiously. _____
17. They established a pre**ced**ent. _____
18. The ex**cise** tax angered the voters. _____
19. It was a **circum**polar voyage. _____
20. The convict's **mal**ediction startled Pip. _____
21. He received the award **post**humously. _____
22. It was not the penult, but the **ante**penult. _____
23. The **sym**metry of the art was boring. _____
24. The judge had to **inter**cede. _____
25. The moon made a **semi**circle. _____

Caesar's English
Cumulative Quiz • Lesson Eight

A. Fill in the definition.
1. placid *calm*
2. grotesque *distorted*
3. sublime *lofty*
4. manifest *obvious*
5. clamor *outcry*
6. odious *hateful*
7. allude *indirectly refer to*
8. acute *sharp*
9. perplex *confuse*
10. prodigious *huge*

B. Write in the Caesar's English word for each definition.
11. friendly *amiable*
12. facial expression *countenance*
13. beautifully made *exquisite*
14. deep *profound*
15. quivering *tremulous*

C. Define the stem that is in **bold**.
16. They began to **scrib**ble furiously. *write*
17. They established a pre**ced**ent. *go*
18. The ex**cise** tax angered the voters. *cut*
19. It was a **circum**polar voyage. *around*
20. The convict's **mal**ediction startled Pip. *bad*
21. He received the award **post**humously. *after*
22. It was not the penult, but the **ante**penult. *before*
23. The **sym**metry of the art was boring. *together*
24. The judge had to **inter**cede. *between*
25. The moon made a **semi**circle. *half*

29

Caesar's English
Lesson Nine

Analogy

REGICIDE : HOMICIDE ::
    a. missive : communication
    b. incredulous : gullible
    c. friendly : furious
    d. malediction : blessing

Answer: a. The first term is a form of the second term; **regicide** is a kind of **homicide**, as a **missive** is a kind of **communication**.

Word Search

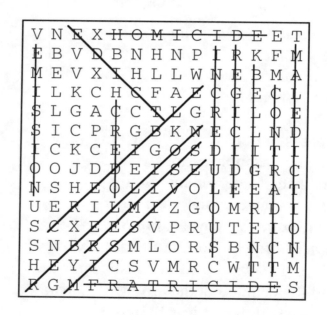

__ INCREDULOUS   __ CREDO   __ CREDIBLE   __ MISSIVE
__ REMISS   __ EMISSION   __ REGICIDE   __ HOMICIDE
__ FRATRICIDE   __ EDICT   __ MALEDICTION   __ CONTRADICT
__ REBELLION   __ BELLICOSE   __ BELLIGERENT

30

Caesar's English
Cumulative Quiz • Lesson Nine

For each sentence, define the stem, not the word, that is in **bold**.

1. The king had his **edict** posted on every wall in town. _____
2. Her **bell**igerent attitude began to make her friends irritable. _____
3. He had to start over because he had been re**miss** in his duties. _____
4. Hard work and constant effort was Benjamin Franklin's **cred**o. _____
5. The Civil War was a great act of national **frat**ricide. _____
6. I con**cede** that you have a good argument. _____
7. Please be **circum**spect in your behavior. _____
8. We reached an **equi**table solution, and everyone was pleased. _____
9. The **ante**bellum period was prosperous. _____
10. The bird and the rhinoceros lived in a **sym**biotic relationship. _____
11. The **inter**stellar space was cold and vast. _____
12. The loud **dis**sonance was harsh on the ears. _____
13. The great old hotel was cruelly **de**molished. _____
14. He glared at her with a **super**cilious scowl. _____
15. She had a weird **pre**monition of approaching danger. _____

For each definition, fill in the Caesar's English word.

16. calm _____
17. skeptical _____
18. confuse _____
19. lofty _____
20. quivering _____

For each Caesar's English word, fill in the definition.

21. amiable _____
22. singular _____
23. grotesque _____
24. odious _____
25. manifest _____

31

Caesar's English
Cumulative Quiz • Lesson Nine

For each sentence, define the stem, not the word, that is in **bold**.

1.   The king had his **e**dict posted on every wall in town. *say*
2.   Her **bell**igerent attitude began to make her friends irritable. *war*
3.   He had to start over because he had been re**miss** in his duties. *send*
4.   Hard work and constant effort was Benjamin Franklin's **cred**o. *believe*
5.   The Civil War was a great act of national **frat**ricide. *brother*
6.   I con**cede** that you have a good argument. *go*
7.   Please be **circum**spect in your behavior. *around*
8.   We reached an **equi**table solution, and everyone was pleased. *equal*
9.   The **ante**bellum period was prosperous. *before*
10. The bird and the rhinoceros lived in a **sym**biotic relationship. *together*
11. The **inter**stellar space was cold and vast. *between*
12. The loud **dis**sonance was harsh on the ears. *away*
13. The great old hotel was cruelly **de**molished. *down*
14. He glared at her with a **super**cilious scowl. *over*
15. She had a weird **pre**monition of approaching danger. *before*

For each definition, fill in the Caesar's English word.

16. calm   *serene*
17. skeptical   *incredulous*
18. confuse   *perplex*
19. lofty   *sublime*
20. quivering   *tremulous*

For each Caesar's English word, fill in the definition.

21. amiable   *friendly*
22. singular   *unique*
23. grotesque   *distorted*
24. odious   *hateful*
25. manifest   *obvious*

Caesar's English
Lesson Ten

Analogies

MELANCHOLY : VISAGE ::

    a. repose : rest
    b. traverse : space
    c. abate : increase
    d. vivid : color

Answer: d. A matter of properties: a **visage** can be **melancholy**, as a **color** can be **vivid**.

STORM : ABATE ::

    a. fear : diminish
    b. traverse : cross
    c. visage : handsome
    d. melancholy : dejected

Answer: a. The second is what the first can do; a **storm** can **abate**, as a **fear** can **diminish**. Furthermore, in each case, the action involves a lessening.

Caesar's English
Cumulative Quiz • Lesson Ten

A. Write in the definition:

1. abate _____
2. visage _____
3. repose _____
4. perplex _____
5. placid _____
6. amiable _____
7. exquisite _____
8. sublime _____
9. manifest _____
10. odious _____

B. Write in the Caesar's English word.

11. sadness _____
12. to respect _____
13. unique _____
14. skeptical _____
15. outcry _____

C. Define the stem in bold.

16. It was a part of their **cred**o. _____
17. I must contra**dict** you. _____
18. He is re**miss** in his duties. _____
19. The state se**cede**d from the Union. _____
20. There was damage to the **ante**rior lobe._____
21. She **inter**jected a comment. _____
22. He felt great **sym**pathy for the family. _____
23. The success was a **pre**lude to triumph. _____
24. The **dis**tortion of facts was intentional. _____
25. She regained her **equi**librium. _____

Caesar's English
Cumulative Quiz • Lesson Ten

A. Write in the definition:
1. abate *to lessen*
2. visage *the face*
3. repose *resting*
4. perplex *to confuse*
5. placid *calm*
6. amiable *friendly*
7. exquisite *beautifully made*
8. sublime *lofty*
9. manifest *obvious*
10. odious *hateful*

B. Write in the Caesar's English word.
11. sadness *melancholy*
12. to respect *venerate*
13. unique *singular*
14. skeptical *incredulous*
15. outcry *clamor*

C. Define the stem in bold.
16. It was a part of their **cred**o. *believe*
17. I must contra**dict** you. *say*
18. He is re**miss** in his duties. *send*
19. The state se**ceded** from the Union. *go*
20. There was damage to the **ante**rior lobe. *before*
21. She **inter**jected a comment. *between*
22. He felt great **sym**pathy for the family. *together*
23. The success was a **pre**lude to triumph. *before*
24. The **dis**tortion of facts was intentional. *away*
25. She regained her **equi**librium. *equal*

Caesar's English
Lesson Eleven

Analogy

OMNIPOTENT : POWER ::

a. omnivorous : teeth

b. omniscient : everything

c. omnivorous : hungry

d. omniscient : knowledge

Answer: d. **Omnipotent** is having all **power** as **omniscient** is having all **knowledge**.

Word Search

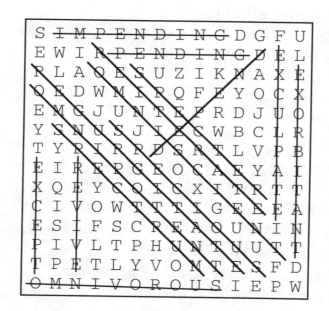

__ SPECTER	__ SPECIOUS	__ SPECTRUM	__ PENDING
__ IMPENDING	__ DEPEND	__ OMNIPOTENT	__ OMNIVOROUS
__ OMNISCIENT	__ REITERATE	__ REGURGITATE	__ REVIVE
__ EXCULPATE	__ EXORBITANT	__ EXCEPT	

Caesar's English
Cumulative Quiz • Lesson Eleven

A. For each sentence, define the stem, not the word, that is in **bold**.
1. Shakespeare's play *Hamlet* has a **spec**ter for a character. _____
2. The im**pend**ing storm made us run for shelter. _____
3. The kid was so smart that she seemed **omni**scient. _____
4. His mother **re**iterated the instructions four times. _____
5. When the real culprit was discovered, Charlie was **ex**culpated. _____
6. The **aqua**tic species thrived in the changing climate. _____
7. Only an **audi**ologist could diagnose the problem. _____
8. The novelist tried to de**scrib**e the scene. _____
9. The South tried to se**cede** from the Union in the Civil War. _____
10. The story was **cred**ible. _____
11. The **circum**stances had changed. _____
12. The **mal**ady was caused by an unknown virus. _____
13. She did **post**graduate work after college. _____
14. The crowd was dis**miss**ed. _____
15. The injury damaged the **ante**rior surface of his brain. _____
16. The wound left the soldier **un**fit for combat duty. _____
17. The two designs formed a perfect **sym**metry. _____
18. The detective investigated the unusual homi**cide**. _____
19. The **dis**pute ended in a happy agreement. _____
20. She drew a **semi**circle on the board. _____
21. The plane began a rapid **de**scent. _____
22. A **bell**icose roar rose from the angry mob. _____
23. The band received a **super**ior rating. _____
24. Captain Nemo navigated the **sub**marine to the South Pole. _____
25. The broken treaty was a **pre**lude to future conflict. _____

B. Define each Caesar's English word.
26. languor _____
27. serene _____
28. acute _____
29. allude _____
30. amiable _____

C. For each definition, fill in the Caesar's English word.
31. confuse _____
32. to lessen _____
33. to respect _____

37

Caesar's English
Cumulative Quiz • Lesson Eleven

A. For each sentence, define the stem, not the word, that is in **bold**.
1. Shakespeare's play *Hamlet* has a **spec**ter for a character. *look*
2. The im**pend**ing storm made us run for shelter. *hang*
3. The kid was so smart that she seemed **omni**scient. *all*
4. His mother **re**iterated the instructions four times. *again*
5. When the real culprit was discovered, Charlie was **ex**culpated. *out*
6. The **aqua**tic species thrived in the changing climate. *water*
7. Only an **audi**ologist could diagnose the problem. *hear*
8. The novelist tried to de**scrib**e the scene. *write*
9. The South tried to se**cede** from the Union in the Civil War. *go*
10. The story was **cred**ible. *believe*
11. The **circum**stances had changed. *around*
12. The **mal**ady was caused by an unknown virus. *bad*
13. She did **post**graduate work after college. *after*
14. The crowd was dis**miss**ed. *away*
15. The injury damaged the **ante**rior surface of his brain. *before*
16. The wound left the soldier **un**fit for combat duty. *not*
17. The two designs formed a perfect **sym**metry. *together*
18. The detective investigated the unusual homi**cide**. *kill*
19. The **dis**pute ended in a happy agreement. *away*
20. She drew a **semi**circle on the board. *half*
21. The plane began a rapid **de**scent. *down*
22. A **bell**icose roar rose from the angry mob. *war*
23. The band received a **super**ior rating. *over*
24. Captain Nemo navigated the **sub**marine to the South Pole. *under*
25. The broken treaty was a **pre**lude to future conflict. *before*

B. Define each Caesar's English word.
26. languor *weakness*
27. serene calm
28. acute *sharp*
29. allude *indirectly refer to*
30. amiable *friendly*

C. For each definition, fill in the Caesar's English word.
31, confuse *perplex*
32. to lessen *abate*
33. to respect *venerate*

38

Analogy

VIVID : PALLID ::
  a. visage : countenance
  b. melancholy : cheerful
  c. undulate : wave
  d. venerate : elder

Answer: b. **Vivid** and **pallid** are opposites, as **melancholy** and **cheerful** are opposites.

Caesar's English
Cumulative Quiz • Lesson Twelve

A. Write in the definition:
1. vulgar _____

2. placid _____
3. serene _____
4. visage _____
5. melancholy _____
6. perplex _____
7. profound _____
8. pallor _____
9. manifest _____
10. abate _____
11. traverse _____
12. repose _____
13. countenance _____
14. clamor _____
15. sublime _____

B. Write in the word defined:
16. quivering _____
17. to wave _____
18. to respect _____
19. hateful _____
20. bright _____
21. friendly _____
22. skeptical _____
23. huge _____
24. distorted _____
25. obvious _____

C. Define the stem in bold.
26. It was a **spec**ious argument. _____
27. They de**pend**ed on her. _____
28. It was a **mal**icious attack. _____
29. All pre**dict**ions were wrong. _____
30. A **bi**lateral agreement is better. _____
31. **Inter**stellar space is cold. _____
32. Do not **equi**vocate with me. _____
33. He is an informed **audi**ophile. _____

Caesar's English
Cumulative Quiz • Lesson Twelve

A. Write in the definition:

1. vulgar *common*
2. placid *calm*
3. serene *calm*
4. visage *the face*
5. melancholy *sadness*
6. perplex *confuse*
7. profound *deep*
8. pallor *paleness*
9. manifest *obvious*
10. abate *to lessen*
11. traverse *to cross*
12. repose *resting*
13. countenance *facial expression*
14. clamor *outcry*
15. sublime *lofty*

B. Write in the word defined:

16. quivering *tremulous*
17. to wave *undulate*
18. to respect *venerate*
19. hateful *odious*
20. bright *vivid*
21. friendly *amiable*
22. skeptical *incredulous*
23. huge *prodigious*
24. distorted *grotesque*
25. obvious *manifest*

C. Define the stem in bold.

26. It was a **spec**ious argument. *look*
27. They de**pend**ed on her. *hang*
28. It was a **mal**icious attack. *bad*
29. All pre**dict**ions were wrong. *say*
30. A **bi**lateral agreement is better. *two*
31. **Inter**stellar space is cold. *between*
32. Do not **equi**vocate with me. *equal*
33. He is an informed **audi**ophile. *hear*

41

Analogy

NOVICE : PERSON ::
a. nova : star
b. beginner : expert
c. new : old
d. child : adult

Answer:a. A **novice** is a kind of **person** who is new, and a **nova** is a kind of **star** that is new.

Word Search

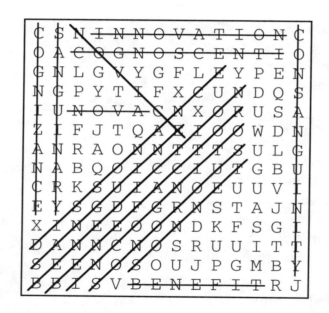

__ BENEFIT	__ BENEDICTION	__ BENEFACTOR	__ SONOROUS
__ DISSONANCE	__ SONNET	__ NOVICE	__ NOVA
__ INNOVATION	__ SANGUINE	__ SANGUINARY	__ CONSANGUINITY
__ COGNIZANCE	__ INCOGNITO	__ COGNOSCENTI	

Caesar's English
Cumulative Quiz • Lesson Thirteen

A. For each sentence, define the stem, not the word, that is in **bold**.
1. Young Pip had no idea who his secret **bene**factor was. _____
2. The creative solution was very in**nov**ative. _____
3. A **son**orous snore issued from the adjacent room. _____
4. According to the fashion **cogn**oscenti, certain colors are stylish. _____
5. We read her brilliant novel with **sangui**ne delight. _____
6. Her mother seemed **omni**scient, and never missed a thing. _____
7. They had to **re**iterate the instructions three times. _____
8. The argument was persuasive, but was unfortunately **spec**ious. _____
9. The convict muttered male**dict**ions as he shrank back. _____
10. The **bell**icose crowd clamored for revenge. _____
11. She was in**cred**ulous at his obvious rudeness. _____
12. The inundation slowly began to re**cede**. _____
13. They tried to **circum**vent the rules. _____
14. The bad guys had **mal**evolent expressions on their faces. _____
15. His answer was not direct, it was **equi**vocal. _____
16. The pronoun disagreed with its **ante**cedent. _____
17. The hero received her award **post**humously. _____
18. He **inter**jected a comment into the discussion. _____
19. They twisted and **dis**torted all of his statements. _____
20. The meal was a **super**b masterpiece. _____
21. The shuttle **de**scended slowly through the clouds. _____
22. The animal was a **bi**ped, like human beings. _____
23. We were **un**able to retort. _____
24. **Sym**pathy is an important quality in a friend. _____
25. The ceremony was a **semi**annual event. _____

B. For each sentence, define the word in **bold**.
26. The **vulgar** behavior offended everyone. _____
27. The hills **undulated** across the landscape. _____
28. The village **venerated** their elderly mayor. _____
29. Finally, the storm began to **abate**. _____
30. His **visage** was sunk in melancholy. _____

C. For each definition, fill in the Caesar's English word.
31. unique _____
32. deep _____
33. to patronize _____

43

Caesar's English
Cumulative Quiz • Lesson Thirteen

A. For each sentence, define the stem, not the word, that is in **bold**.
1. Young Pip had no idea who his secret **bene**factor was. *good*
2. The creative solution was very in**nov**ative. *new*
3. A **son**orous snore issued from the adjacent room. *sound*
4. According to the fashion **cogn**oscenti, certain colors are always stylish. *know*
5. We read her brilliant novel with **sangui**ne delight. *blood*
6. Her mother seemed **omni**scient, and never missed a thing. *all*
7. They had to **re**iterate the instructions three times. *again*
8. The argument was persuasive, but was unfortunately **spec**ious. *look*
9. The convict muttered male**dict**ions as he shrank back. *say*
10. The **bell**icose crowd clamored for revenge. *war*
11. She was in**cred**ulous at his obvious rudeness. *believe*
12. The inundation slowly began to re**cede**. *go*
13. They tried to **circum**vent the rules. *around*
14. The bad guys had **mal**evolent expressions on their faces. *bad*
15. His answer was not direct, it was **equi**vocal. *equal*
16. The pronoun disagreed with its **ante**cedent. *before*
17. The hero received her award **post**humously. *after*
18. He **inter**jected a comment into the discussion. *between*
19. They twisted and **dis**torted all of his statements. *away*
20. The meal was a **super**b masterpiece. *over*
21. The shuttle **de**scended slowly through the clouds. *down*
22. The animal was a **bi**ped, like human beings. *two*
23. We were **un**able to retort. *not*
24. **Sym**pathy is an important quality in a friend. *together*
25. The ceremony was a **semi**annual event. *half*

B. For each sentence, define the word in **bold**.
26. The **vulgar** behavior offended everyone. *common*
27. The hills **undulated** across the landscape. *to wave*
28. The village **venerated** their elderly mayor. *to respect*
29. Finally, the storm began to **abate**. *to lessen*
30. His **visage** was sunk in melancholy. *face*

C. For each definition, fill in the Caesar's English word.
31. unique *singular*
32. deep *profound*
33. to patronize *condescend*

44

Caesar's English
Lesson Fourteen

Analogies

SAGACIOUS : PROPHET ::
a. verbal : writer
b. victim : martyr
c. prostrate : upright
d. articulate : mute

Answer: a. A question of characteristics pertaining to something. A prophet can be sagacious, as a writer can be verbal.

REMONSTRATE : AGREE ::
a. sagacity : wisdom
b. abyss : ocean
c. subtle : obvious
d. vex : irritate

Answer: c. These are opposites; to **remonstrate** is the opposite of to **agree**, as **subtle** is the opposite of **obvious**.

Caesar's English
Cumulative Quiz • Lesson Fourteen

A. Write in the definition:

1. tedious _____
2. undulate _____
3. sagacity _____
4. clamor _____
5. repose _____
6. serene _____
7. subtle _____
8. abate _____
9. wistful _____
10. amiable _____
11. allude _____
12. sublime _____
13. perplex _____

B. Write in the Caesar's English word for each definition.

14. unique _____
15. to cross _____
16. to object _____
17. quivering _____
18. common _____
19. obvious _____
20. huge _____
21. distorted _____
22. hateful _____
23. sharp _____

C. Define the stem in **bold**.

24. The quadruped was an **omni**vore. _____
25. I was asked to **re**state the question. _____
26. The Romans watched the **spect**acle in the Colosseum. _____
27. She gave the vale**dict**ory speech. _____
28. He had a **bell**igerent attitude. _____
29. It was the night of the vernal **equi**nox. _____
30. The lesion was on the **ante**rior lobe of the brain. _____
31. She penned an pleasant **post**script. _____
32. The **inter**view lasted three hours. _____
33. The motion was for immediate **dis**missal. _____

46

Caesar's English
Cumulative Quiz • Lesson Fourteen

A. Write in the definition:
1. tedious *boring*
2. undulate *to wave*
3. sagacity *wisdom*
4. clamor *outcry*
5. repose *resting*
6. serene *calm*
7. subtle *slight*
8. abate *to lessen*
9. wistful *yearning*
10. amiable *friedly*
11. allude *indirectly refer to*
12. sublime *lofty*
13. perplex *to confuse*

B. Write in the Caesar's English word for each definition.
14. unique *singular*
15. to cross *traverse*
16. to object *remonstrate*
17. quivering *tremulous*
18. common *vulgar*
19. obvious *manifest*
20. huge *prodigious*
21. distorted *grotesque*
22. hateful *odious*
23. sharp *acute*

C. Define the stem in **bold**.
24. The quadruped was an **omni**vore. *all*
25. I was asked to **re**state the question. *again*
26. The Romans watched the **spec**tacle in the Colosseum. *look*
27. She gave the vale**dict**ory speech. *say*
28. He had a **bell**igerent attitude. *war*
29. It was the night of the vernal **equi**nox. *equal*
30. The lesion was on the **ante**rior lobe of the brain. *before*
31. She penned an pleasant **post**script. *after*
32. The **inter**view lasted three hours. *between*
33. The motion was for immediate **dis**missal. *away*

47

Analogy

DEJECTION : MOOD ::
a. dispute : agreement
b. verdict : decision
c. magnanimous : small-minded
d. verify : report

Answer: b. **Dejection** is a kind of **mood**, as a **verdict** is a kind of **decision**.

Word Search

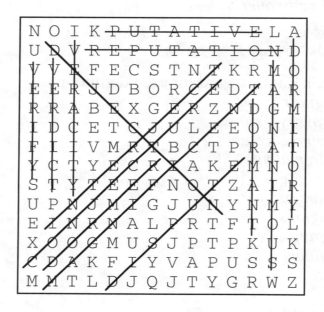

```
N O I K P U T A T I V E L A
U D V R E P U T A T I O N D
V V F E C S T N K R M O
E E R U D B O R C E D T A R
R R A B E X G E R Z N D G M
I D C E T J U L E E O N I
F I V M R B C T P R A T
Y C T Y E C K A K E M N O
S T Y E E N O T Z A I R
U P N M I G J U N Y N M Y
E I R N A L R T F T O L
X O O G M U S J P T P K U K
C D A K F Y V A P U S S S
M M T L D J Q J T Y G R W Z
```

__ DEJECTION   __ INTERJECT   __ CONJECTURE   __ DORMANT
__ DORMITORY   __ DORMER   __ MAGNATE   __ MAGNIFICENT
__ MAGNANIMOUS   __ VERIFY   __ VERACITY   __ VERDICT
__ DISPUTE   __ PUTATIVE   __ REPUTATION

Caesar's English
Cumulative Quiz • Lesson Fifteen

A. For each sentence, define the stem, not the word, that is in **bold**.
1. The jury brought back a **ver**dict of "not guilty." _____
2. There was a light in one of the high **dorm**er windows. _____
3. He was the **put**ative leader of a crime organization. _____
4. The **magn**animous winner congratulated her opponent. _____
5. "May I inter**ject** a comment?" he asked politely. _____
6. The star traveled in**cogn**ito, with a false beard and big hat. _____
7. The beautiful **son**net took the poet two months to write. _____
8. For this effort, I would like to have your **bene**diction. _____
9. The **sangui**nary battle roared on for three days. _____
10. The **omni**vorous creatures ate everything in sight. _____
11. The innocent man was **ex**culpated by the court. _____
12. The scientist studied the **spec**trum of the star. _____
13. He suddenly received a **miss**ive from his fiance. _____
14. The detective specialized in homi**cide**s. _____
15. "Winning isn't everything," was their **cred**o. _____
16. The **audi**ence listened attentively. _____
17. The Romans built the **aque**duct from the mountains to the city. _____
18. Magellan **circum**navigated the globe. _____
19. The painful **mal**ady lasted for months. _____
20. **Post**erity will always remember Rachel Carson. _____
21. The **sym**metry of the building was boring. _____
22. An **inter**national relief effort helped the refugees. _____
23. We were **dis**tracted by the constant noise. _____
24. The seal **sub**merged below the surface of the sea. _____
25. They **super**vised the playground carefully. _____

B. For each word, write in the definition.
26. sagacity _____
27. undulate _____
28. prodigious _____
29. condescend _____
30. exquisite _____

C. For each definition, supply the Caesar's English word.
31. friendly _____
32. to lessen _____
33. paleness _____

Caesar's English
Cumulative Quiz • Lesson Fifteen

A. For each sentence, define the stem, not the word, that is in **bold**.
1. The jury brought back a **ver**dict of "not guilty." *true*
2. There was a light in one of the high **dorm**er windows. *sleep*
3. He was the **put**ative leader of a crime organization. *think*
4. The **magn**animous winner congratulated her opponent. *great*
5. "May I inter**ject** a comment?" he asked politely. *throw*
6. The star traveled in**cogn**ito, with a false beard and big hat. *know*
7. The beautiful **son**net took the poet two months to write. *sound*
8. For this effort, I would like to have your **bene**diction. *good*
9. The **sangui**nary battle roared on for three days. *blood*
10. The **omni**vorous creatures ate everything in sight. *all*
11. The innocent man was **ex**culpated by the court. *out*
12. The scientist studied the **spec**trum of the star. *look*
13. He suddenly received a **miss**ive from his fiance. *send*
14. The detective specialized in homi**cide**s. *kill*
15. "Winning isn't everything," was their **cred**o. *believe*
16. The **audi**ence listened attentively. *hear*
17. The Romans built the **aque**duct from the mountains to the city. *water*
18. Magellan **circum**navigated the globe. *around*
19. The painful **mal**ady lasted for months. *bad*
20. **Post**erity will always remember Rachel Carson. *after*
21. The **sym**metry of the building was boring. *together*
22. An **inter**national relief effort helped the refugees. *between*
23. We were **dis**tracted by the constant noise. *away*
24. The seal **sub**merged below the surface of the sea. *under*
25. They **super**vised the playground carefully. *over*

B. For each word, write in the definition.
26. sagacity   *wisdom*
27. undulate   *to wave*
28. prodigious   *huge*
29. condescend   *to patronize*
30. exquisite   *beautifully made*

C. For each definition, supply the Caesar's English word.
31. friendly   *amiable*
32. to lessen   *abate*
33. paleness   *pallor*

Caesar's English
Lesson Sixteen

Analogy

VEX : IRRITATE ::
    a. tedious : lecture
    b. articulate : speak
    c. sagacity : dullness
    d. subtle : change

Answer: b. These terms are synonyms; to **vex** is to **irritate**, as to **articulate** is to **speak**.

Caesar's English
Cumulative Quiz • Lesson Sixteen

A. Write in the definition:
1. tedious _____
2. undulate _____
3. sagacity _____
4. clamor _____
5. vulgar _____
6. serene _____
7. subtle _____
8. abate _____
9. wistful _____
10. amiable _____
11. articulate _____
12. abyss _____
13. martyr _____
14. prostrate _____
15. vex _____

B. Write in the Caesar's English word.
16. paleness _____
17. to cross _____
18. to object _____
19. quivering _____
20. bright _____

C. Define the stem in bold.
21. Her testimony had obvious **ver**acity. _____
22. The symptoms were **dorm**ant for a year. _____
23. The de**put**ation arrived. _____
24. The wealthy **magn**ate greeted the powerful potentate. _____
25. We were thoroughly de**ject**ed. _____
26. I wasn't **cogn**izant of the real reason. _____
27. They decided to call the company **Son**y. _____
28. Her famous **bene**volence benefitted everyone. _____
29. His **sangui**ne good will made him many friends. _____
30. The Roman gods were not **omni**potent. _____
31. The **exit** is on the left. _____
32. The argument was convincing but entirely **spec**ious. _____
33. The **miss**iles were aimed at the enemy. _____

Caesar's English
Cumulative Quiz • Lesson Sixteen

A. Write in the definition:
1. tedious *boring*
2. undulate *to wave*
3. sagacity *wisdom*
4. clamor *outcry*
5. vulgar *common*
6. serene *calm*
7. subtle *slight*
8. abate *to lessen*
9. wistful *yearning*
10. amiable *friendly*
11. articulate *to express clearly*
12. abyss *a bottomless depth*
13. martyr *one who suffers*
14. prostrate *lying down*
15. vex *to irritate*

B. Write in the Caesar's English word.
16. paleness *pallor*
17. to cross *traverse*
18. to object *remonstrate*
19. quivering *tremulous*
20. bright *vivid*

C. Define the stem in bold.
21. Her testimony had obvious **ver**acity. *true*
22. The symptoms were **dorm**ant for a year. *sleep*
23. The de**put**ation arrived. *think*
24. The wealthy **magn**ate greeted the powerful potentate. *great*
25. We were thoroughly de**ject**ed. *throw*
26. I wasn't **cogn**izant of the real reason. *know*
27. They decided to call the company **Son**y. *sound*
28. Her famous **bene**volence benefitted everyone. *good*
29. His **sangui**ne good will made him many friends. *blood*
30. The Roman gods were not **omni**potent. *all*
31. The **ex**it is on the left. *out*
32. The argument was convincing but entirely **spec**ious. *look*
33. The **miss**iles were aimed at the enemy. *send*

53

Analogy

BIOGRAPHY : CHRONOLOGICAL ::
   a. chronic : brief
   b. autograph : signature
   c. autocracy : monarchy
   d. counting : sequential

Answer: d. **Biography** is in **chronological** order; **counting** is in **sequential** order.

Word Search

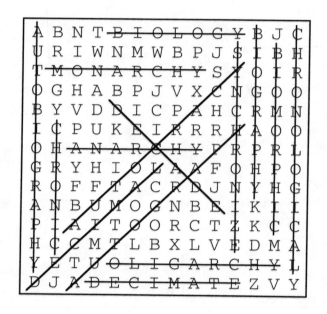

```
A B N T B I O L O G Y B J C
U R I W N M W B P J S I B H
T M O N A R C H Y S X O I R
O G H A B P J V X C N G O O
B Y V D I C P A H C R M N N
I C P U K E I R R H A O O O
O H A N A R C H Y P R P R L
G R Y H I O L A A F O H P O
R O F F T A C R D J N Y H G
A N B U M O G N B E I K I I
P I A I T O O R C T Z K C C
H C C M T L B X L V E D M A
Y E T U O L I G A R C H Y L
D J A D E C I M A T E Z V Y
```

__ MONARCHY   __ OLIGARCHY   __ ANARCHY   __ BIOLOGY
__ BIOGRAPHY   __ BIOMORPHIC   __ AUTOGRAPH   __ AUTOCRACY
__ AUTOBIOGRAPHY   __ CHRONIC   __ CHRONOLOGICAL   __ SYNCHRONIZE
__ DECADE   __ DECIMAL   __ DECIMATE

Caesar's English
Cumulative Quiz • Lesson Seventeen

For each sentence, define the stem, not the word, that is in **bold**.

1. He carefully read the wonderful **auto**biography. _____
2. Alexander the Great **dec**imated the Persian army. _____
3. Crazy an**archy** seized the great city. _____
4. The huge sculpture in the park was curvy and **bio**morphic, not angular. ___
5. The **chron**ic cough lingered through the month.
6. She muttered not a blessing but a **male**diction. _____
7. The animals lived together in a happy **sym**biosis. _____
8. Magellan wanted to **circum**navigate the earth. _____
9. The company was hired to **de**molish the old building. _____
10. She added a **post**script to the long letter. _____
11. They blasted off into **inter**stellar space. _____
12. He **equi**vocated, trying not to answer the question. _____
13. The **audi**ence listened to the Mozart concerto. _____
14. A **bell**icose roar erupted from the great mob. _____
15. She pre**dict**ed the eclipse using mathematics. _____
16. Rosalind Franklin's work earned the re**spec**t of other scientists. _____
17. The **pre**lude introduced the theme of the music. _____
18. She nailed the oak planks down to the **sub**floor. _____
19. His **super**fluous comments bored the listeners. _____
20. The **dis**pute, though serious, never became angry. _____
21. In the **ante**bellum period, citizens did not know the war was coming. _____
22. We were in**cred**ulous over her ridiculous denials. _____
23. She applied to the law school's ad**miss**ions department. _____
24. Curiously, the **aqua**rium was full of tadpoles. _____
25. She re**cogn**ized the Picasso painting immediately. _____

For each word, write the definition.

26. abyss _____
27. martyr _____
28. traverse _____
29. vex _____

For each definition, write the word.

30. express clearly _____
31. lying down _____
32. obvious _____

55

Caesar's English
Cumulative Quiz • Lesson Seventeen

For each sentence, define the stem, not the word, that is in **bold**.
1. He carefully read the wonderful **auto**biography. *self*
2. Alexander the Great **dec**imated the Persian army. *ten*
3. Crazy an**archy** seized the great city. *government*
4. The huge sculpture in the park was curvy and **bio**morphic, not angular. *life*
5. The **chron**ic cough lingered through the month. *time*
6. She muttered not a blessing but a **mal**ediction. *bad*
7. The animals lived together in a happy **sym**biosis. *together*
8. Magellan wanted to **circum**navigate the earth. *around*
9. The company was hired to **de**molish the old building. *down*
10. She added a **post**script to the long letter. *after*
11. They blasted off into **inter**stellar space. *between*
12. He **equi**vocated, trying not to answer the question. *equal*
13. The **audi**ence listened to the Mozart concerto. *hear*
14. A **bell**icose roar erupted from the great mob. *war*
15. She pre**dict**ed the eclipse using mathematics. *say*
16. Rosalind Franklin's work earned the re**spec**t of other scientists. *look*
17. The **pre**lude introduced the theme of the music. *before*
18. She nailed the oak planks down to the **sub**floor. *under*
19. His **super**fluous comments bored the listeners. *over*
20. The **dis**pute, though serious, never became angry. *away*
21. In the **ante**bellum period, citizens did not know the war was coming. *before*
22. We were in**cred**ulous over her ridiculous denials. *believe*
23. She applied to the law school's ad**miss**ions department. *send*
24. Curiously, the **aqua**rium was full of tadpoles. *water*
25. She re**cogn**ized the Picasso painting immediately. *know*

For each word, write the definition.
26. abyss *bottomless depth*
27. martyr *one who suffers*
28. traverse *to cross*
29. vex *to irritate*

For each definition, write the word.
30. express clearly *articulate*
31. lying down *prostrate*
32. obvious *manifest*

56

Analogies

APPREHENSION : EMOTION ::
  a. superfluous : verbose
  b. martyr : hero
  c. stolid : unemotional
  d. palpable : tangible

Answer: b. The first is a form of the second. **Apprehension** is a kind of B, as a **marty** is one kind of **hero**.

Caesar's English
Cumulative Quiz • Lesson Eighteen

A. Write in the definition:
1. apprehension _____
2. lurid _____
3. tangible _____
4. vex _____
5. austere _____
6. acute _____
7. remonstrate _____
8. abyss _____
9. martyr _____
10. undulate _____

B. Write in the word defined:
11. huge _____
12. spread throughout _____
13. indirectly refer to _____
14. extra _____
15. facial expression _____
16. deep _____
17. wisdom _____
18. quivering _____
19 skeptical _____
20. to lessen _____

C. Define the Latin stem in **bold**.
21. Many great thinkers are **auto**didacts. _____
22. The **dec**imal system is clear. _____
23. The new nation was a modified mon**archy**. _____
24. They paddled through **Bio**luminescent Bay in Puerto Rico. _____
25. For lack of a marine **chron**ometer, many ships were lost. _____
26. The **mal**evolent phantom slithered through the night. _____
27. The **sym**pathetic vibrations were perfectly synchronized. _____
28. The in**spect**ion is always thorough. _____
29. My **pre**decessor was famous for long lunches. _____
30. The **sub**tle influences made a difference. _____
31. Our **super**natural beliefs alter our view of reality. _____
32. The Soviet **dis**sidents were led away to prison. _____
33. The **pre**position's antecedent was unknown. _____

58

Caesar's English
Cumulative Quiz • Lesson Eighteen

A. Write in the definition:
1. apprehension   *fear*
2. lurid   *sensational*
3. tangible   *touchable*
4. vex   *to irritate*
5. austere   *bare*
6. acute   *sharp*
7. remonstrate   *to object*
8. abyss   *bottomless depth*
9. martyr   *one who suffers*
10. undulate   *to wave*

B. Write in the word defined:
11. huge   *prodigious*
12. spread   *throughout*
13. indirectly   *refer to*
14. extra   *superfluous*
15. facial   *expression*
16. deep   *profound*
17. wisdom   *sagacity*
18. quivering   *tremulous*
19 skeptical   *incredulous*
20. to lessen   *abate*

C. Define the Latin stem in **bold**.
21. Many great thinkers are **auto**didacts. *self*
22. The **dec**imal system is clear. *ten*
23. The new nation was a modified mon**archy**. *government*
24. They paddled through **Bio**luminescent Bay in Puerto Rico. *life*
25. For lack of a marine **chron**ometer, many ships were lost. *time*
26. The **mal**evolent phantom slithered through the night. *bad*
27. The **sym**pathetic vibrations were perfectly synchronized. *together*
28. The in**spect**ion is always thorough. *look*
29. My **pre**decessor was famous for long lunches. *before*
30. The **sub**tle influences made a difference. *under*
31. Our **super**natural beliefs alter our view of reality. *over*
32. The Soviet **dis**sidents were led away to prison. *away*
33. The **pre**position's antecedent was unknown. *before*

59

Analogy

NEOPHYTE : VETERAN ::
a. telescope : microscope
b. geography : earth
c. introduction : book
d. geometry : mathematics

Answer: A **neophyte** is the opposite of a **veteran**, as a **telescope** is the opposite of a **microscope**.

Word Search

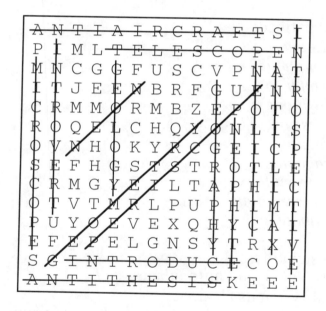

__ GEOGRAPHY	__ GEOLOGY	__ GEOMETRY	__ TELESCOPE
__ MICROSCOPE	__ PERISCOPE	__ ANTIAIRCRAFT	__ ANTICLIMAX
__ ANTITHESIS	__ INTRODUCE	__ INTROSPECTIVE	__ INTROVERT
__ NEON	__ NEOLITHIC	__ NEOPHYTE	

Caesar's English
Cumulative Quiz • Lesson Nineteen

A. For each sentence, define the stem, not the word, that is in **bold**.
1. The **neo**phyte didn't even know where to begin. _____
2. The outcome was the **anti**thesis of what they had intended. _____
3. He felt sad and **intro**spective the whole day, and barely spoke. _____
4. The **geo**logy course taught her about the different kinds of rocks. _____
5. She used the new electron **micro**scope in the science lab. _____
6. The **auto**didact had educated himself. _____
7. A **dec**ade passed before the wildlife returned. _____
8. The mon**archy** passed peacefully to the new king. _____
9. The lengthy **bio**graphy of Churchill was a pleasure to read. _____
10. She felt **sym**pathy for the earthquake victims she read about. _____
11. The **circum**spect spy was never arrested. _____
12. The banker accepted the large **de**posit. _____
13. In the United States, *ex **post** facto* laws are illegal. _____
14. The court issued an **inter**diction to stop the drilling. _____
15. The **equi**lateral triangle had three sides the same length. _____
16. She won first chair after her great performance at the **audi**tion. _____
17. The beautiful **pre**lude lasted nearly six minutes. _____
18. The Romans loved a good **spec**tacle. _____
19. "We all live in a yellow **sub**marine," he said. _____
20. The lunchroom was carefully **super**vised. _____

B. Define the word.
21. pervade _____
22. apprehension _____
23. lurid _____
24. tangible _____
25. abyss _____
26. vex _____
27. wistful _____

C. Supply the word defined.
28. to object _____
29. wisdom _____
30. boring _____
31. distorted _____
32. confuse _____
33. to respect _____

61

Caesar's English
Cumulative Quiz • Lesson Nineteen

A. For each sentence, define the stem, not the word, that is in **bold**.
1. The **neo**phyte didn't even know where to begin. *new*
2. The outcome was the **anti**thesis of what they had intended. *against*
3. He felt sad and **intro**spective the whole day, and barely spoke. *into*
4. The **geo**logy course taught her about the different kinds of rocks. *earth*
5. She used the new electron **micro**scope in the science lab. *small*
6. The **auto**didact had educated himself. *self*
7. A **dec**ade passed before the wildlife returned. *ten*
8. The mon**archy** passed peacefully to the new king. *government*
9. The lengthy **bio**graphy of Churchill was a pleasure to read. *life*
10. She felt **sym**pathy for the earthquake victims she read about. *together*
11. The **circum**spect spy was never arrested. *around*
12. The banker accepted the large **de**posit. *down*
13. In the United States, *ex **post** facto* laws are illegal. *after*
14. The court issued an **inter**diction to stop the drilling. *between*
15. The **equi**lateral triangle had three sides the same length. *equal*
16. She won first chair after her great performance at the **audi**tion. *hear*
17. The beautiful **pre**lude lasted nearly six minutes. *before*
18. The Romans loved a good **spec**tacle. *look*
19. "We all live in a yellow **sub**marine," he said. *under*
20. The lunchroom was carefully **super**vised. *over*

B. Define the word.
21. pervade   *spread throughout*
22. apprehension   *fear*
23. lurid   *sensational*
24. tangible   *touchable*
25. abyss   *bottomless depth*
26. vex   *irritate*
27. wistful   *yearning*

C. Supply the word defined.
28. to object   *remonstrate*
29. wisdom   *sagacity*
30. boring   *tedious*
31. distorted   *grotesque*
32. confuse   *perplex*
33. to respect   *venerate*

Analogies

TANGIBLE : PALPABLE ::
a. austere : ascetic
b. superfluous : insufficient
c. stolid : visage
d. genial : aloof

Answer: a. These are synonyms. **Palpable** means **tangible**; **austere** can mean **ascetic**.

THIEF : FURTIVE ::
a. stolid : effusive
b. palpable : manifest
c. odor : pervade
d. monastery : austere

Answer: d. The second is a characteristic of the first. A **thief** is **furtive**, as a **monastery** is **austere**.

Caesar's English
Cumulative Quiz • Lesson Twenty

A. Write in the definition:
1. furtive _____
2. lurid _____
3. tangible _____
4. palpable _____
5. austere _____
6. acute _____
7. remonstrate _____
8. abyss _____
9. one who suffers _____
10. to wave _____

B. Write in the word defined:
11. unemotional _____
12. spread through _____
13. anxiety _____
14. extra _____
15. kind _____
16. deep _____
17. wisdom _____
18. quivering _____
19. skeptical _____
20. to lessen _____

C. Define the stem in bold.
21. They named the discovery **neo**n. _____
22. She took a strong **anti**histamine. _____
23. The long **intro**duction put everyone to sleep. _____
24. The satellite was in **geo**synchronous orbit. _____
25. **Micro**biotic species filled the pond water. _____
26. He had become a stoic **auto**maton. _____
27. There were three **deca**liters of fluid. _____
28. The hier**archy** were rarely consulted. _____
29. A strong anti**bio**tic saved her life. _____
30. **Sym**biotic species help us digest our food. _____
31. The **circum**stances are different now. _____
32. The conditions are **de**plorable. _____
33. Wait until the **post**-election reports are in. _____

64

Caesar's English
Cumulative Quiz • Lesson Twenty

A. Write in the definition:
1. furtive *stealthy*
2. lurid *sensational*
3. tangible *touchable*
4. palpable *touchable*
5. austere *bare*
6. acute *sharp*
7. remonstrate *to object*
8. abyss *a bottomless depth*
9. martyr *one who suffers*
10. undulate *to wave*

B. Write in the word defined:
11. unemotional *stolid*
12. spread through *pervade*
13. fear *apprehension*
14. extra *superfluous*
15. kind *genial*
16. deep *profound*
17. wisdom *sagacity*
18. quivering *tremulous*
19. skeptical *incredulous*
20. to lessen *abate*

C. Define the stem in bold.
21. They named the discovery **neo**n. *new*
22. She took a strong **anti**histamine. *against*
23. The long **intro**duction put everyone to sleep. *into*
24. The satellite was in **geo**synchronous orbit. *earth*
25. **Micro**biotic species filled the pond water. *small*
26. He had become a stoic **auto**maton. *self*
27. There were three **deca**liters of fluid. *ten*
28. The hier**archy** were rarely consulted. *government*
29. A strong anti**bio**tic saved her life. *life*
30. **Sym**biotic species help us digest our food. *together*
31. The **circum**stances are different now. *around*
32. The conditions are **de**plorable. *down*
33. Wait until the **post**-election reports are in. *after*

65

Caesar's English
Twenty Questions - Lessons 1-5

1. What did James M. Barrie write?

2. What is the English cognate of the Spanish soberbio?

3. What Roman Emperor said, "I must feed my poor"?

4. Who said, "The die is cast"?

5. Who wrote *Dr. Jekyll and Mr. Hyde*?

6. Jonathan Swift is the author of what famous book?

7. What state is Cross Creek in?

8. Who said that "Knowledge itself is power"?

9. An advanced word that means *to put between* is...

10. Who wrote *Wuthering Heights*?

11. What emperor sent a mother a message?

12. Cato said that what must be destroyed?

13. Caesar wrote that the Gauls were getting reinforcements from whom?

14. What deserts a falling building, according to Pliny?

15. Nero's ruins gave us what word?

16. Who wrote *The Wind in the Willows?*

17. A word that means the opposite is called what?

18. What does *circumspect* mean?

19. What Roman Emperor warned against condemning the innocent?

20. Who said, "It is certain because it is impossible"?

Caesar's English
Twenty Questions - Lessons 1-5

1. What did James M. Barrie write? Peter Pan
2. What is the English cognate of the Spanish soberbio? superb
3. What Roman Emperor said, "I must feed my poor"? Vespasian
4. Who said, "The die is cast"? Caesar
5. Who wrote *Dr. Jekyll and Mr. Hyde*? Robert Louis Stevenson
6. Jonathan Swift is the author of what famous book? Gulliver's Travels
7. What state is Cross Creek in? Florida
8. Who said that "Knowledge itself is power"? Francis Bacon
9. An advanced word that means *to put between* is... interpose
10. Who wrote *Wuthering Heights*? Emily Brontë
11. What emperor sent a mother a message? Titus
12. Cato said that what must be destroyed? Carthage
13. Caesar wrote that the Gauls were getting reinforcements from whom? Britain
14. What deserts a falling building, according to Pliny? the mice
15. Nero's ruins gave us what word? grotesque
16. Who wrote *The Wind in the Willows*? Kenneth Grahame
17. A word that means the opposite is called what? an antonym
18. What does *circumspect* mean? cautious, careful
19. What Roman Emperor warned against condemning the innocent? Trajan
20. Who said, "It is certain because it is impossible"? Tertullian

Caesar's English
Twenty Questions - Lessons 6-10

1. What did Charles Dodgson write?

2. What structure brought Romans their water?

3. Where did Roman Christians bury their dead?

4. What was Octavian's other name?

5. What did Watson and Crick discover?

6. Who wrote *The Secret Garden*?

7. Who wrote *Pride and Prejudice*?

8. What does *bellicose* mean?

9. What word means full of disbelief?

10. Who won the 1993 Nobel Prize for Literature?

11. What Stoic philosopher said to read good books many times?

12. Who described "the scowling visage of Chingachgook"?

13. What word means, good looking but false?

14. Who wrote *A Midsummer Night's Dream*?

15. Tacitus advised us to think of our ancestors and what else?

16. Who said there is nothing surprising in the Gauls' readiness to revolt?

17. Where was Seneca born?

18. Who wrote *The Yearling*?

19. Who said that the fatherland is the common parent of us all?

20. Who wrote books signed, "By a Lady"?

Caesar's English
Twenty Questions - Lessons 6-10

1. What did Charles Dodgson write? Alice in Wonderland

2. What structure brought Romans their water? the aqueduct

3. Where did Roman Christians bury their dead? in the catacombs

4. What was Octavian's other name? Augustus

5. What did Watson and Crick discover? the structure of DNA

6. Who wrote *The Secret Garden*? Frances Hodgson Burnett

7. Who wrote *Pride and Prejudice*? Jane Austen

8. What does *bellicose* mean? warlike

9. What word means full of disbelief? incredulous

10. Who won the 1993 Nobel Prize for Literature? Toni Morrison

11. What Stoic philosopher said to read good books many times? Seneca

12. Who described "the scowling visage of Chingachgook"? James Fennimore Cooper

13. What word means, good looking but false? specious

14. Who wrote *A Midsummer Night's Dream*? William Shakespeare

15. Tacitus advised us to think of our ancestors and what else? our posterity

16. Who said there is nothing surprising in the Gauls' readiness to revolt? Caesar

17. Where was Seneca born? Spain

18. Who wrote *The Yearling*? Marjorie Kinnan Rawlings

19. Who said that the fatherland is the common parent of us all? Cicero

20. Who wrote books signed, "By a Lady"? Jane Austen

Caesar's English
Twenty Questions - Lessons 11-15

1. What does *omnipotent* mean?
2. What word means good-looking but false?
3. Who wrote *Robinson Crusoe*?
4. What general led elephants over the Alps?
5. Who said, "Dulce et decorum est pro patria mori?
6. What famous novel did Sir Walter Scott write?
7. What is Marguerite Annie Johnson's other name?
8. Who read a poem at President John Kennedy's inauguration?
9. Who wrote *The Red Badge of Courage*?
10. What does *cognizant* mean?
11. Does *sanguine* mean bloody?
12. In what century did Geoffrey Chaucer write?
13. Laberius said "He must fear many, whom many fear" about whom?
14. Who wrote *The Call of the Wild*?
15. Who died, calling himself an artist?
16. What word means generous and noble in thought?
17. What word describes our sad, down-thrown spirit?
18. What book was translated into twenty languages?
19. What Roman philosphers taught us not to skim when reading?
20. We know Mary Ann Evans by what literary name?

Caesar's English
Twenty Questions - Lessons 11-15

1. What does *omnipotent* mean? all-powerful

2. What word means good-looking but false? specious

3. Who wrote *Robinson Crusoe*? Daniel Defoe

4. What general led elephants over the Alps? Hannibal

5. Who said, "Dulce et decorum est pro patria mori? Horace

6. What famous novel did Sir Walter Scott write? *Ivanhoe*

7. What is Marguerite Annie Johnson's other name? Maya Angelou

8. Who read a poem at President John Kennedy's inauguration? Robert Frost

9. Who wrote *The Red Badge of Courage*? Stephen Crane

10. What does *cognizant* mean? aware, knowing

11. Does *sanguine* mean bloody? no, it means cheerful

12. In what century did Geoffrey Chaucer write?   the 14th

13. Laberius said "He must fear many, whom many fear" about whom? Caesar

14. Who wrote *The Call of the Wild*? Jack London

15. Who died, calling himself an artist? Nero

16. What word means generous and noble in thought?   magnanimous

17. What word describes our sad, down-thrown spirit? dejection

18. What book was translated into twenty languages? *Uncle Tom's Cabin*

19. What Roman philosphers taught us not to skim when reading? the Stoics

20. We know Mary Ann Evans by what literary name? George Eliot

Caesar's English
Twenty Questions - Lessons 16-20

1. How did the Pantheon get its name?

2. What word meant leaderless in Greek?

3. Rachel Carson warned against what substance?

4. Who invited his horse to dinner?

5. Who wrote *Silas Marner*?

6. Vercingetorix was able to defeat whom in battle?

7. Who said that superfluous wealth only buys superfluities?

8. What biological word means beginner?

9. What writer went to the Alaskan Gold Rush?

10. Who created the first newspapers?

11. What word comes from a Latin word for thief?

12. Who moved from Manchester, England, to Knoxville, Tennesee?

13. Who wrote *Little Lord Fauntleroy*?

14. Who said that people should be judged by their minds?

15. What does *Acta Diurna* mean?

16. Who wrote *The Time Machine*?

17. Who wrote *Walden*?

18. Who said the Gauls are hasty and impetuous in war?

19. What did Mary Shelley write?

20. Who became the editor of the *Westminster Review*?

Caesar's English
Twenty Questions - Lessons 16-20

1. How did the Pantheon get its name? it was build in honor of all (pan) gods (theo)

2. What word meant leaderless in Greek? anarchy, anarchios

3. Rachel Carson warned against what substance? DDT

4. Who invited his horse to dinner? Caligula

5. Who wrote *Silas Marner*? George Eliot

6. Vercingetorix was able to defeat whom in battle? *Caesar*

7. Who said that superfluous wealth only buys superfluities? Henry David Thoreau

8. What biological word means beginner? neophyte

9. What writer went to the Alaskan Gold Rush? Jack London

10. Who created the first newspapers? Caesar

11. What word comes from a Latin word for thief? furtive

12. Who moved from Manchester, England, to Knoxville, Tennesee? Frances Hodgson Burnett

13. Who wrote *Little Lord Fauntleroy*? Frances Hodgson Burnett

14. Who said that people should be judged by their minds? Seneca

15. What does *Acta Diurna* mean? Daily Deeds

16. Who wrote *The Time Machine*? H.G. Wells

17. Who wrote *Walden*? Henry David Thoreau

18. Who said the Gauls are hasty and impetuous in war? *Caesar*

19. What did Mary Shelley write? *Frankenstein*

20. Who became the editor of the *Westminster Review*? George Eliot